DAILY MOTIVATION TO BUILD THE
LIFE YOU WANT

THE SOMEDAY

(IS NOT A DAY IN THE WEEK)

JOURNAL

SAM HORN

MY DAD THOUGHT HE had time. He worked six-seven days a week most of his adult life.

He was an honorable man who felt a deep obligation to make an enduring difference for people. He achieved that goal. But at a cost.

Dad's dream was to visit all the National Parks. He finally took off on his long-delayed dream a week after he retired.

A week after that, he had a stroke in a hotel bathroom.

He never got to visit Bryce, Banff or Zion. He never got to do what he had dreamed of doing his whole life.

I don't want that to happen to me. I don't want that to happen to you.

I don't want that to happen to anyone.

Yet while interviewing people for my SOMEDAY is Not a Day in the Week book, many people told me all the things they plan (hope?) to do...someday.

Whether it's to ask for a promotion or project they think they deserve, spend more time with their family, take better care of themselves, or pursue a passion project–they told me they'd do it when they're not so busy, when they retire, when they have more money... fill in the blank.

That's a prescription for regret.

The good news is, you don't need to win the lottery or walk away from your responsibilities to make your life more of what you want it to be.

There are things you can do right here, right now to live an authentic life that's more in alignment with your values.

There are mini-actions you can do on a daily basis to be happier, healthier and more fulfilled. That's the purpose of this journal.

THE POWER OF WRITING THINGS DOWN

"Write it on your heart that every day
is the best day of the year."
–Ralph Waldo Emerson

THERE'S SOMETHING TANGIBLY POWERFUL about writing things–not just on your heart–but in a journal. That's not just my opinion.

The Royal College of Psychiatrists found that "Expressive writing–often connected with journalling–is especially therapeutic." It not only helps you make sense of your life, it can reduce stress, improve mood, and even cause you to heal faster from injuries and surgeries.

There's another reason that taking even 5 minutes to journal is a good investment in a quality life. Did you see the movie "As Good as It Gets" with Jack Nicholson and Helen Hunt?

At one point, she looks at him and says, "Pay me a compliment, Melvin." He says, "That's a pretty dress."

She says, "No, pay me a real compliment."

He seems to sense their relationship hangs on his ability to say something personally meaningful. He digs deep and comes up with, "You make me want to be a better man."

My hope is that the quotes in this journal make you want to be a better person.

My hope is they help you be more alert to what's right in your world–and help you see your life and the people in it with more appreciative eyes.

This journal can be a written witness to your life. A record of your days.

Instead of time flying by, you'll NOTICE the days, SEE the blessings, and RECORD them so you can revisit them whenever you want, as often as you want.

I hope this journal is Day One of the rest of your life–and that it helps you create the quality of life you want, need and deserve starting today, not someday.

Ready? Let's go.

JANUARY

"There are always flowers for those
who want to see them."
—Matisse

THIS QUOTE FROM MATISSE sums up my life philosophy.

How about you? Do you choose to see flowers–no matter what?

That's one of the purposes of this SOMEDAY journal. To help you see flowers – what's right in the world–and write it down so you can reinforce it and remember it.

And if it's winter, or you're in a city and don't see flowers, maybe you can be a flower.

Compliment someone on a job well done. Give a stranger a smile. Reach out to a new co-worker and invite them to join you for lunch.

May this journal be a garden of flowers you can return to whenever you want a reminder of the beauty that exists around us if we choose to see it and be it.

JANUARY

1

"If you've made a decision and haven't taken action, you haven't really made a decision."
—*Tony Robbins*

Decide right now that THIS is going to be the best year of your life. What is one action you're going to take today to help make that happen?

Notes

_____

_____

_____

_____

_____

JANUARY

2

"Life is too short to live the same day twice."
—Jennifer Lopez

Do your days run together? Does today look just like yesterday which was like the day before that? Today, do something different. Make the day count instead of allowing it to be same-old, same-old.

Notes

JANUARY

3

"*Tell me, what is it you plan to do*
with your one wild and precious life?"
—*Mary Oliver*

When you were growing up, what did you plan to do with your wild and precious life? What did you want to be? What did you dream of doing? How closely does your life match your plans?

Notes

_____

_____

_____

_____

_____

JANUARY

4

*"Serendipity is no accident.
It's our best future meeting us halfway."*
—Sam Horn

Some people feel serendipity "the phenomenon of finding valuable or agreeable things unintentionally" is a coincidence, a happy accident. Have you had a "stroke of good luck" happen "out of the blue" that beat the odds?

Notes

_____

_____

_____

_____

_____

JANUARY

5

"Happiness consists of living each day
as if it were the first day of your honeymoon
and the last day of your vacation."
—Leo Tolstoy

Tolstoy said this more than 150 years ago, and yet it is as applicable today as it was then. How will you live today as if it was the first day of your honeymoon and the last day of your vacation?

Notes

_____

_____

_____

_____

_____

JANUARY

"The earth laughs in flowers."
—Ralph Waldo Emerson

Today, treat yourself to a flower. It doesn't even have to be a bouquet. It can be one rose, one lily. Put it by your desk, your bed, in your kitchen where it brightens your soul and your day.

Notes

_____

_____

_____

_____

_____

JANUARY

7

"Follow your soul. It knows the way."
—Rumi

Trying to make a decision? Your soul knows the way. What is it whispering to you?

Notes

_____

_____

_____

_____

_____

JANUARY

"I imagine that YES is the only living thing."
—e.e. cummings

Today you will get an offer or a nudge to try something. The critic that lives on your shoulder may start telling you all the reasons you "can't" do this. Ignore the critic. Say YES.

Notes

_____

_____

_____

_____

_____

JANUARY

9

"Nobody sees a flower really, it is so small.
We haven't time, and to see takes time."
—Georgia O'Keefe

What a powerful reminder to take the time to really see someone or something with appreciative eyes. The moment we really SEE anything, we are flooded with gratitude. Grace is available anytime we want... for a moment's notice.

Notes

_____

_____

_____

_____

_____

JANUARY

10

"Happiness is when what you think,
say, and do are in harmony."
—Gandhi

Would you say your life is in harmony? If so, why? If not, why not?

Notes

_____

_____

_____

_____

_____

JANUARY
11

*"When I ask people, 'What does happiness
mean to you?' I often get long pauses and blank looks.
If we can't define what happiness means to us, how are
we supposed to know it when
we experience it?"*
—Sam Horn

How about you? How would you define happiness?

Notes

_____

_____

_____

_____

_____

JANUARY

12

"The stories we tell ourselves are
what make our dreams come true."
—Sheri Salata

What's your dream? What is something you'd like to happen by the end of this year? What story are you telling yourself about it? Is that story helping or hurting your chances of it happening?

Notes

_____

_____

_____

_____

_____

JANUARY

13

"God can really show off when she wants to."
—Anne Lamott

Too often, we focus on the traffic, how late we are, or that someone is in our way. Today, look up and around. How is God showing off today? How can you imprint and absorb her miracles?

Notes

_____

_____

_____

_____

_____

JANUARY

14

"Life moves pretty fast. If you don't stop and look around once in a while, you could miss it."
—*Ferris Bueller*

If you were going to play hooky for a day – or for an hour – what would you do?

Notes

_____

_____

_____

_____

_____

JANUARY

15

*When Ferris Bueller's friends ask what
they'll do with their day of hooky, he says "The
question isn't what are we are going to do? The
question is, what aren't we going to do?"*

What won't you do on your day – or hour – of hooky?

Notes

_____

_____

_____

_____

_____

JANUARY

16

"If our instincts alert us when something's about to go wrong, don't they also alert us when something is about to go right? If we have a sixth sense that alerts us to dissonance, don't we also have a sixth sense that alerts us to resonance?"
—Sam Horn

Today, keep your antenna up for when something feels wrong and when something feels right. Your instincts have your best interests at heart. Pay attention to them. Honor them.

Notes

_____

_____

_____

_____

_____

JANUARY

17

"Remember how far you've come,
not how far you have to go."
—Rick Warren

Do you have a project that's taking a long time? Can you focus on how far
you've come instead of on how far you have to go?

Notes

_____

_____

_____

_____

_____

JANUARY

18

*"It's the people who don't ask questions
who remain clueless."*
—Neil Degrasse Tyson

The rest of this month features questions that can give you clues into what's contributing to your quality of life – what's compromising it. First question? On a Scale of 1-10, how happy are you?

Notes

_____

_____

_____

_____

_____

JANUARY

19

*"We're here for a reason. I believe a bit
of the reason is to throw little torches out
to lead people through the dark."*
—Whoopi Goldberg

Who is someone who has contributed to your happiness? Who has "thrown you a torch to lead you through the dark?" What has that person done to mentor you, support you, inspire you?

Notes

_____

_____

_____

_____

_____

JANUARY

20

"Stay away from negative people.
They have a problem for every solution."
—Albert Einstein

Who is someone who has compromised your happiness? What has that person done to cause problems for you or make you feel bad and/or unworthy?

Notes

_____

_____

_____

_____

_____

JANUARY

21

*"There is no such thing as fun for
the whole family."*
—Jerry Seinfeld

What was your family like growing up? Was it fun or not so much? What did your parents model for you and/or teach you?

How did your siblings treat you? How does that impact you now?

Notes

_____

_____

_____

_____

_____

JANUARY

22

"It is never too late to be what
you might have been."
—*George Eliot*

Fill in this sentence, "If it weren't too late, I'd. (What? Travel more? Start my own business? Search for my soul mate?) Why do you believe it's too late? Is that true?

Notes

_____

_____

_____

_____

_____

JANUARY

23

"There's no happier person
than a truly thankful person."
—Joyce Meyers

Who is someone you know who is happy? Why do you think they are?
Be specific.

Notes

_____

_____

_____

_____

_____

JANUARY

24

"Simplicity is the greatest sophistication."
—*Leonardo da Vinci*

"If I were to right-size my life and stuff, I would let goof." What's preventing you from simplifying, releasing, quitting getting rid of, or clearing that up?

Notes

_____

_____

_____

_____

_____

JANUARY

25

"Don't tell me where your priorities are.
Show me where you spend your money and I'll tell
you what they are."
—James W. Frick

Finish this sentence, "Money is." How would you describe your financial situation? How much money do you need/want to be comfortable and/or feel secure?

Notes

_____

_____

_____

_____

_____

JANUARY

26

*"It is health that is real wealth
and not pieces of gold and silver."*
—Gandhi

Let's talk about your body. Are you fit, physically active, sick, in pain? On a scale of 1-10, how would you rate your health? How would you rate your body image? How is that impacting your overall quality of life?

Notes

_____

_____

_____

_____

_____

JANUARY

27

"Desire is the secret to a successful career.
Not education. Not being born with
hidden talents. Desire."
—Johnny Carson

On a scale of 1-10 ,how fulfilled are you by your work? What do you like about it? What don't you like about it? Are you in the right job, right career? Explain your answer

Notes

_____

_____

_____

_____

_____

JANUARY

28

*"If you ask me what I came to do
in this world, I, an artist, will answer you:
I am here to live out loud."*
—*Emile Zola*

Have you ever had a calling? Something you felt you came to do in this world? Did you pursue that dream, passion project? If so, how did that turn out for you?

Notes

_____

_____

_____

_____

_____

JANUARY

29

"Today is the only life you are sure of.
Make the most of it. Get interested in something.
Shake yourself awake. Develop a hobby. Let the winds
of enthusiasms weep through you.
Live with gusto."
—Dale Carnegie

What do you do for fun? Do you have a hobby? A special interest? What shakes you awake–helps you live with gusto?

Notes

_____

_____

_____

_____

_____

JANUARY

30

"I'm hanging in there, trying to spend
as much quality time with my wife and kids as
possible, there's a great satisfaction in knowing that
I'm walking off the field with no regrets."
—Randy Pausch, The Last Lecture

Do you have a regret? Something you wish you could go back and change?
What is it? Is it too late for a do-over?

Notes

_____

_____

_____

_____

_____

JANUARY

31

"Looking back at my life's voyage,
I can only say that it has been a golden trip."
—Ginger Rogers

Was there a time in your life you were really happy? What was going on at that time that contributed to that being a "golden time"?

Notes

_____

_____

_____

_____

_____

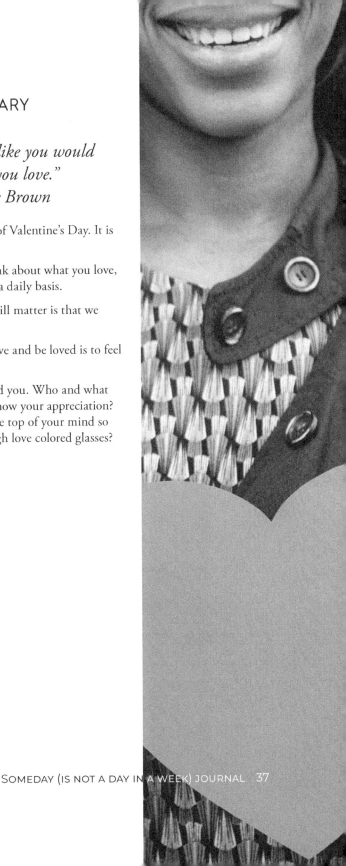

FEBRUARY

"Talk to yourself like you would
to someone you love."
—*Brene Brown*

Fᴇʙʀᴜᴀʀʏ ɪꜱ ᴛʜᴇ ᴍᴏɴᴛʜ of Valentine's Day. It is the month of love.

Throughout this month, think about what you love, who you love, and why... on a daily basis.

At the end of our life, what will matter is that we loved and were loved.

As David Viscott says,"To love and be loved is to feel the sun from both sides".

On a daily basis, look around you. Who and what do you love? How can you show your appreciation? How can you keep love at the top of your mind so you can see the world through love colored glasses?

FEBRUARY

1

"The life you've led doesn't need to be
the only life you have."
—Anna Quindlen

Look at the question from yesterday. What is one thing that contributed to you being happy then? How will you start to bring more of that into your life – starting today?

Notes

_____

_____

_____

_____

FEBRUARY

2

"If you're searching for that one person who will
change your life, look in the mirror."
—Roman Price

Right now, get up and go over and look in a mirror. Do you like the person you see? If so, why so? If not, Why not?

Notes

_____

_____

_____

_____

_____

FEBRUARY

3

"Maturity is arriving at a sense of enoughness."
—David Whyte

Do you feel you are enough? Or do you feel you're not good enough- that you aren't enough? What contributes to this?

Notes

_____

_____

_____

_____

_____

FEBRUARY

*"If your compassion does not include
yourself, it is incomplete."*
—Jack Kornfield

Are you hard on yourself? Are you your own worst critic? Today, show yourself
the same compassion you show others.

Notes

_____

_____

_____

_____

_____

FEBRUARY

5

"No one can figure out your worth but you."
—Pearl Bailey

In the past, did other people's approval determine your self-worth? Who?
Your parents? Partner? Coach or teacher? How so? Who determines your
self-worth now?

Notes

_____

_____

_____

_____

_____

FEBRUARY

"I take care of me. I'm the only one I've got."
—Groucho Marx

On a scale of 1 – 10, how well are you taking care of you?

What is something you will do today that comes under the heading of
"self-care?"

Notes

_____

_____

_____

_____

_____

FEBRUARY

"I am in love with hope."
—Mitch Albom

When Mitch Albom closed his keynote at the Maui Writers Conference with this quote, everyone in the audience rose to their feet and gave him a standing ovation. How about you? Would you say you're in love with hope? Why or why not?

Notes

_____

_____

_____

_____

_____

FEBRUARY

"Above all, be the heroine of your life,
not the victim."
—Nora Ephron

What is the story of your life? Do you dwell on a dysfunctional family?

A messy breakup or difficult divorce? That doesn't need to define you unless you let it. What is a NEW story you will start telling yourself today? A story where you are the hero or heroine, not the victim?

Notes

_____

_____

_____

_____

_____

FEBRUARY

9

"Don't let them tame you."
—Isadora Duncan

Has someone in your life tried to tame you? Why did they want to control you, diminish you? Were they jealous, threatened, possessive? As Colette said, "The better we feel about ourselves, the fewer times we have to knock someone down to feel tall. "Were they trying to keep you small so they could feel tall?

Notes

_____

_____

_____

_____

_____

FEBRUARY

10

"Be brave enough to be your true self."
—*Queen Latifah*

Would you say you're your "true self?" Why or why not?

Notes

_____

_____

_____

_____

_____

FEBRUARY

11

"It's not your job to like me; it's mine."
—*Byron Katie*

Do you know anyone who bases their self-worth on whether other people like them? Do you see how that means their self-esteem is always dependent on where they are, who they're with?

Notes

_____

_____

_____

_____

_____

FEBRUARY

12

*"Many people feel their worth as a
human being is proportional to what they
have achieved in their life."*
—*Dr. David Burns*

Sound like anyone you know? What are your thoughts about this? What do you think your worth depends on?

Notes

_____

_____

_____

_____

_____

FEBRUARY

13

"I shake off everything when I write.
My sorrows disappear. My courage is reborn."
—Anne Frank

Okay, you have been writing in this journal for more than one month now. Does focusing on the good things in your life help you make your sorrows disappear? Does it rebirth your courage? What impact is your daily practice of journalling having on you?

Notes

_____

_____

_____

_____

_____

FEBRUARY

14

"A loving heart is the truest wisdom."
—Charles Dickens

Valentine's Day is not just about flowers and boxes of chocolate. It is about expressing the love you have in your heart. Why not take five minutes to write a note saying exactly what it is you love most about a special someone? Chances are your handwritten note will mean more than anything money could buy.

Notes

_____

_____

_____

_____

_____

FEBRUARY

15

"Our soul-mate is the person who
makes life come to life."
—Richard Bach

Who is your soul-mate? Who makes life come to life for you?

Notes

_____

_____

_____

_____

_____

FEBRUARY

16

"Love is not a permanent state of enthusiasm."
—*Esther Perel*

Do you agree with Esther's insight? Do you think it's unrealistic to stay wildly in love with a romantic partner over the years? Would it be healthier if we accepted that it's natural to have a waning of enthusiasm? If you have a significant other in your life, what feeling has replaced enthusiasm over time?

Notes

_____

_____

_____

_____

_____

FEBRUARY

17

*"The essence of charm is the ability to
lose yourself in the other person."*
—*Eleanor Roosevelt*

Will you be meeting someone new this week? You can overcome shyness or set aside nervousness by asking "Tell me" questions. Instead of "Did you have a good vacation?" Say, "Tell me about your vacation."

"Tell me" gives people a hook on which to hang a conversation.

Notes

_____

_____

_____

_____

_____

FEBRUARY

18

"Live in day-tight compartments."
—*Dale Carnegie*

Promise yourself you will live in "day- RIGHT" compartments." Do one thing
for you everyday to make your day feel right. What is that for you? To kiss your
kids? To read by your favorite window? To greet the day with a hot cup of tea?
To do something nice for someone?

Notes

_____

_____

_____

_____

_____

FEBRUARY

19

*"When we get too caught up in the
busyness of the world, we lose connection with
one another and with ourselves."*
—Jack Kornfield

If you find yourself getting caught up in the busyness of the world today, stop,
look around, reconnect with someone or something by seeing them with
fresh eyes. The connection you seek is available anytime you want… for a
moment's notice.

Notes

_____

_____

_____

_____

_____

FEBRUARY

20

*"When we are unable to find tranquility within
ourselves,it is useless to seek it elsewhere."*
—La Rochefoucauld

Know someone who says, "That person makes me mad?" Other people don't
make us mad. We are the one who continues to think about what they did that
was unfair or undeserved. Instead, tell yourself, "Let it go, let it go." Re-find
your tranquility by focusing on someone you love.

Notes

_____

_____

_____

_____

_____

FEBRUARY

21

*"Someone asked what I regarded as the most
important requirements for happiness. My answer:
A feeling you have been honest with yourself and those
around you, a feeling you have done the best you could
in your personal life and work,
and the ability to love others."*
—*Eleanor Roosevelt*

What are your three most important requirements of happiness?

Notes

_____

_____

_____

_____

_____

FEBRUARY

22

"Two of the most important words in any relationship?
FRESH START."
—Sam Horn

Are you upset with someone or is someone upset with you? Instead of carrying a grudge or allowing the resentment to fester, look at the person today and say, "FRESH START?"

Notes

_____

_____

_____

_____

_____

FEBRUARY

22

"When you can't keep up, connect."
—Mary Loverde

My long-time friend Mary Loverde, author of "I Used to Have a Handle on Life, But It Broke," believes the best remedy for stress is to reach out and connect with someone we love. Who will you spend quality time with today to counteract a stressful situation?

Notes

_____

_____

_____

_____

_____

FEBRUARY

23

"25% of all resolutions have fallen by the way side by the second week of the new year."
—New York Times article by David DeSteno

We're 7 weeks into the new year. Have you kept your resolutions? Which ones? If so, congrats. If not, why did they fall by the wayside?

Notes

_____

_____

_____

_____

_____

FEBRUARY

24

*"The minute you settle for less than you deserve, you
get even less than you settled for."*
—Columnist Maureen Dowd

Are you asking for or negotiating something? Are you compromising what you
want before you even say a word? Resolve to ask for what you want, need and
deserve – nothing less.

Notes

_____

_____

_____

_____

_____

FEBRUARY

25

"Every woman needs a room of her own."
—*Virginia Woolf*

Are you around people all day every day? Do you crave a room of your own? If so, carve out some private time today.

Notes

_____

_____

_____

_____

_____

FEBRUARY

26

*"Stories were full of hearts broken by love,
but what really broke a heart, was taking away its
dream, whatever that dream might be."*
—*Pearl S. Buck*

Do you have a dream that's been taken away from you? What is that?

Notes

_____

_____

_____

_____

_____

FEBRUARY

27

"Jealousy is just love and hate at the same time."
—Drake

What a provocative quote. He's right. When we are jealous it's because we want what someone else is or has.

Notes

_____

_____

_____

_____

_____

"One day, you're going to wake up and there won't be any time left to do the things you've always wanted to do."

—*Paulo Coelho*

MARCH

SOME PEOPLE THINK IT'S morbid to think of our mortality. I think it's motivating. John Kotter from Harvard says the #1 precursor to change is a sense of urgency. That makes sense, doesn'ti t?

If we think we have all the time in the world, it's easy to procrastinate.

It is when we're aware the clock is ticking that we're motivated to make the most of our time now... not someday.

This month, approach each day with a sense of urgency.

Instead of assuming that what you want to do will be waiting for you when you're ready for it, do something to set it in motion this month, this week, today.

You will never regret making time for who and what's important to you. You will only regret not doing it...sooner.

MARCH

1

"The future is already here
and we're already late."
—John Legend

What is something you hope or plan to do… in the future? How can you set that in motion today instead of waiting for a future that may never come?

Notes

_____

_____

_____

_____

_____

MARCH

2

"The question you should be asking isn't, 'What are my goals?' but 'What would excite me?'"
—*Tim Ferriss*

So, what would excite you? What is one thing you could achieve or receive that would put the light on in your eyes?

Notes

_____

_____

_____

_____

_____

MARCH

3

"When people abandon their goals, it's not always for lack of inspiration; it's for lack of accountability."
—*Xander Schultz, CEO of Complete App*

What is a goal you want to achieve by the end of this month? How will you hold yourself accountable for it so you successfully achieve it?

Notes

_____

_____

_____

_____

_____

MARCH

4

*"My parents told me I wouldn't amount to
anything because I procrastinated so much.
I told them, 'Just you wait.'"*
—Judy Tenuta

What is something you want or need to do – but you keep putting it off?
Procrastination kills self-esteem. How will you take one step towards doing
that today?

Notes

_____

_____

_____

_____

_____

MARCH
5

"Life, as it is called, is for most of us
one long postponement."
—Henry Miller

What is something else you've been postponing that needs to be done? Do yourself a favor. Even if you've been dreading it, take one action to address it. You'll feel better.

Notes

_____

_____

_____

_____

_____

MARCH

*"Is there ever any particular spot where one can put
one's finger and say, 'It all began that day, at such a
time and such a place, with such an incident?'"*
—*Agatha Christie*

Many people tell me their biggest time waste is scrolling social media. Make today the spot you change that. When will you set aside your device and use that time for a higher priority?

Notes

_____

_____

_____

_____

_____

MARCH

7

"Things don't get better by chance,
they get better by change."
—Jim Rohn

What is one thing you wish was different about your life? It won't get better by chance. What is one thing you will do today to jump-start that change?

Notes

_____

_____

_____

_____

_____

MARCH

"How we spend our days is, of course,
how we spend our lives."
—Annie Dillard

A single mother with a full-time job and two small kids told me she's just "trying to get through the day." Please understand, there are no throw- away days. How will you make today count?

Notes

_____

_____

_____

_____

_____

MARCH

9

"You don't have to see the whole staircase,
just take the first step."
—Martin Luther King Jr.

What is something you want to do, but you can't see the whole staircase, so you've been waiting for clarity? Taking the first step will kick-start the clarity more than waiting will.

Notes

_____

_____

_____

_____

_____

MARCH

10

"At the moment of truth,
there are either reasons or results."
—Chuck Yeager

Look ahead. What is one thing you would regret not doing? How will you prevent that regret by addressing this, fixing this, acting on this… this week?

Notes

_____

_____

_____

_____

_____

MARCH

11

"People in my survey report they're too busy to make friends outside the office, too busy to date, sleep, have lunch, even too busy to have sex."
—EricBarkerinTime.com

I am embarrassed to say I lived twenty minutes from a long time friend in Washington DC, and we only saw each other a few times a year because we were "too busy." We finally rectified that and avoided a regret by arranging monthly walk-talks. Who is a friend you'll reach out to today?

Notes

_____

_____

_____

_____

_____

MARCH

12

"Now is the new later."
—Sam Horn

What is something you've promised a friend you'll do later? Could you pleasantly surprise them and yourself and set it in motion today? Could you call about it, jump online and register for it, pay for it?

Notes

_____

_____

_____

_____

_____

MARCH

13

"I didn't come this far to only come this far."
—sign in gym

Running low on willpower, self-discipline or determination? Repeat this mantra to yourself, "I didn't come this far to only come this far."

Notes

_____

_____

_____

_____

_____

MARCH

14

*"I have learned never to ask whether
you can do something. Say, instead, that you are doing
it. Then fasten your seat belt. The most remarkable
things follow."*
—Julia Cameron

Today, instead of asking or wondering whether you can do something, just do it.

Notes

_____

_____

_____

_____

_____

MARCH

15

*"They say time changes things, but you
actually have to change them yourself."*
—Andy Warhol

What is something you hope will get better? How will you kick-start that
change today instead of waiting for it to happen on its own?

Notes

_____

_____

_____

_____

_____

MARCH

16

*"I'm not having a mid-life crisis.
I'm having mid- life clarity."*
—Sam Horn

When I announced my Year by the Water, most people said, "Take me with you." But one person was concerned I was having a mid-life crisis. I told her, "Actually, I'm having mid-life clarity." How about you? What are you getting clarity about?

Notes

_____

_____

_____

_____

_____

MARCH

17

*"Knowing what you want out of life
means nothing if you can't also say no to the
things that fill your life but not your soul."*
—*Jonathan Fields*

Who or what will you say NO to today – so you open up space for something more meaningful?

Notes

_____

_____

_____

_____

_____

MARCH

18

"I'm no longer accepting the things I cannot change. I am changing the things I cannot accept."
—Angela Davis

What is something you're no longer willing to accept? How will you start changing it today?

Notes

_____

_____

_____

_____

_____

MARCH

19

"You have got to own your days and live them, each one of them, everyone of them, or else the years go by and none of them belong to you."
—Herb Gardner

Do you feel you're "owning" your days? Or do you feel your life is not your own? Explain.

Notes

_____

_____

_____

_____

_____

MARCH

20

"We can't be that kid standing at the top
of the waterslide, overthinking it. You
have to go down the chute."
—Tina Fey

What have you been wanting to do? Are you over-thinking it? Today's the day
you–whoosh-go down the water-slide.

Notes

_____

_____

_____

_____

_____

MARCH

21

"When you take one step towards God,
God takes ten steps towards you."
—Sufi saying

Trying to make a decision and don't know what to do? What feels right in your heart? Take one step towards that and God—or the Universe or Providence or whatever you prefer to call it—will take ten steps towards you.

Notes

_____

_____

_____

_____

_____

MARCH

22

"It takes guts to get out of ruts."
—Robert H. Schuller

What is a rut you're in – something you do mindlessly and repeatedly – with no payoff?

Notes

_____

_____

_____

_____

_____

MARCH

23

"I have heard every excuse in the book,
except a good one."
—*Bob Greene*

What is something you really want to change – but you keep coming up with reasons (aka excuses) for not doing it? What if you got rid of those excuses and started it… today?

Notes

_____

_____

_____

_____

_____

MARCH

24

"I am not the product of my circumstances;
I'm the product of my decisions."
—Stephen R. Covey

Do you know someone who is still blaming their parents for what's wrong with their life? Even if they had a tough childhood, they can use those circumstances as an excuse or as incentive. What circumstances are impacting you? What have you decided to do about them?

Notes

_____

_____

_____

_____

_____

MARCH

25

*"I want to live my days so my nights
are not filled with regrets."*
—D. H. Lawrence

What is a habit that you wish you didn't have? A habit that would lead to regrets
if you continue doing it?

Notes

_____

_____

_____

_____

_____

MARCH

26

"It seems as if the second half of a man's life is made up of nothing but the habits he accumulated during the first half."
—*Fyodor Dostoyevsky*

What is a habit you're happy you have? A habit that contributes to your quality of life?

Notes

_____

_____

_____

_____

MARCH

27

"I'm not telling you it will be easy.
I'm telling you it will be worth it."
—Art Williams

Fast-forward to the end of this year. Fill in this sentence, "I am so glad I am no longer _____. It wasn't easy changing _____, however I am _____ now that I have."

Notes

_____

_____

_____

_____

_____

MARCH

28

"I'm always outside my comfort zone."
—Tory Burch

What does this quote mean to you? How will you try something new–do something for the first time that's outside your comfort zone–today?

Notes

_____

_____

_____

_____

_____

MARCH

29

*"We always experience anxiety whenever we confront
the potential of our own development."*
—Soren Kierkegaard

Anxiety is a GOOD THING. It means you're stretching yourself and moving
out of your comfort zone. That's where the growth is. What is one thing you'll
do today – e.g., talk to someone new, go somewhere by yourself or speak up at a
staff meeting – that makes you anxious?

Notes

_____

_____

_____

_____

_____

MARCH

30

*"In baseball and in business, there are three types of
people. Those who make it happen, those who watch it
happen and those who wonder what happened."*
—*Tommy Lasorda*

I believe there are four types of people. Those who make things happen, those
who watch what happens, those who wonder what happens, and those who
partner with what wants to happen. We've been taught to plan life. Today, how
will you partner with life?

Notes

_____

_____

_____

_____

MARCH

31

"There is no present like the time."
—Sam Horn

Each day you're gifted with 24 hours. How will you be more present to how you spend it today?

Notes

_____

_____

_____

_____

_____

*"People can't jump on your bandwagon if it's
parked in the garage."*
—Sam Horn

APRIL

WHAT IS SOMETHING YOU want to start, change or launch?

That idea, project or dream isn't doing anyone any good sitting in your head.

There are people out there who could encourage you, mentor you, make connections for you, perhaps even fund you... but you've got to give them a chance.

This month, share your idea with colleagues. Talk out your dream with a trusted friend.

Sign up for a class, workshop or support group so you can brainstorm, strategize and learn how to move this forward.

Remember the African proverb, "If you want to go fast, go alone. If you want to go far, go together."

APRIL

1

"Until you're ready to look foolish,
you'll never have the possibility of being great."
—Cher

Food for thought this April Fool's Day. What do you think Cher means in this quote? Do you agree? When is a time you dared to look or act foolish? What happened as a result?

Notes

_____

_____

_____

_____

_____

APRIL

2

"Anything is possible if you have the
right people supporting you."
—Misty Copeland

Would you say you have the right people supporting you? Who is someone who believes in you, who has encouraged you? How so?

Notes

_____

_____

_____

_____

_____

APRIL

3

"You can't connect the dots looking forward;
you can only connect them looking backwards.
You have to trust the dots will somehow
connect in your future."
—Steve Jobs

We're being sent dots all the time. Dots are congruent ideas, opportunities, and individuals. We're supposed to pay attention to the ones that resonate, collect them, connect them and act on them. When we do, we set our SerenDestiny (a life where the light is on in our eyes) in motion.

Notes

_____

_____

_____

_____

_____

APRIL

4

"Let me listen to me, not to them."
—Gertrude Stein

Who are you listening to about a goal that's important to you? Are they pointing out all the ways this could go wrong? Is it time remove this naysayer from your life or remove yourself from theirs?

Notes

_____

_____

_____

_____

_____

APRIL

5

"The worst enemy to creativity is self-doubt."
—Sylvia Plath

What is something you'd like to try, but self-doubts are getting in your way?
What are you doubting? That you could succeed? Are those doubts helping
or hurting?

Notes

_____

_____

_____

_____

_____

APRIL

"Kindness has not left the building."
—Seth Godin

Do you agree? Who is someone at your job who has been kind to you?

Notes

_____

_____

_____

_____

_____

APRIL

7

"In influencing others, example is not
the main thing; it's the only thing."
—*Albert Schweitzer*

Who is someone who has positively influenced you? What did that person do or
say that has impacted you?

Notes

_____

_____

_____

_____

_____

APRIL

"When someone shows you who they are;
believe them the first time."
—Maya Angelou

Please think of a naysayer who seems to put obstacles in your path whenever you try to do something important to you. Ask yourself these questions.

Is it this person's "nature" to be cautious and careful? Do they think it is their role or responsibility to "look out for you" and save you from danger or risk?

Is this a one-time incident or an ongoing issue? Does this person have a pattern of trying to "hold you back" or is their input specific to this particular situation?

Play out what would happen if you heed this person's warnings and don't do what you want to do. Is it possible you would thank them in the long run? Or would you feel defeated and deflated, like you abandoned a dream that was meaningful to you?

Is it worth trying to have an honest, two-way conversation with this person or are they locked into their point of view? Will it do any good to try to resolve this situation with them or is it wiser to move on and connect with people who will help move this forward?

APRIL

9

"No person is your friend who denies
your right to grow."
—Alice Walker

What did you conclude after asking yourself the questions from yesterday?
Is this person trying to help you grow or do they see your growth as a threat?
What are you going to do about it?

Notes

_____

_____

_____

_____

_____

APRIL

10

"Everyone shines, given the right lighting."
—Susan Cain

Who is someone who has shone a light on you? Who has celebrated your achievements? Who has encouraged you, believed in you, given you an opportunity to shine?

Notes

_____

_____

_____

_____

_____

APRIL

11

"Perfectionism is another spelling
for procrastination."
—*T-shirt slogan*

Waiting to get something out in the world because it's not perfect? Please remind yourself, "Better fine than perfect."

Notes

_____

_____

_____

_____

_____

APRIL

12

*"The future belongs to those who believe in the beauty
of their dreams."*
—Eleanor Roosevelt

A man in a SOMEDAY salon told me he was working two jobs and "too busy
to dream." I asked, "How can you have a dream come true if you don't have
a dream?" Even if you're busy, write down a dream you want to come true. It
doesn't cost anything yet it can mean everything.

Notes

_____

_____

_____

_____

APRIL

13

"Teachers affect eternity.
Who knows where their influence will end?"
—Henry Brooks Adams

Who is a teacher who positively influenced you? What did that teacher do or say to have enduring impact on you?

Notes

_____

_____

_____

_____

_____

APRIL

14

"A leader is one who knows the way,
goes the way, and shows the way."
—John C. Maxwell

Who is a leader you respect? Someone who knows the way, goes the way, and shows the way?

Notes

_____

_____

_____

_____

_____

APRIL

15

"I think writers are too worried it's all been said
before. Sure it has, but not by you."
—Asha Dornfest

If you're hesitating to share your story or lessons-learned because you're afraid
they're not original, please understand they may be the right words at the right
time for the right person. Stories and lessons-learned don't help anyone in
your head.

Notes

_____

_____

_____

_____

_____

APRIL

16

*"We are all looking for someone
who will make us do what we can."*
—Ralph Waldo Emerson

Who is someone who "made you" do what you're capable of? Someone who stretched you, challenged you, held you accountable? Maybe you didn't even like this person at the time, but you now feel indebted to them for helping you be the person you wanted to be?

Notes

_____

_____

_____

_____

_____

APRIL

17

"Optimism is a happiness magnet."
—Mary Lou Retton

Who is the most optimistic person you know? How does their optimism affect their quality of life? How does it affect you?

Notes

_____

_____

_____

_____

_____

APRIL

18

"Quiet people have the loudest minds."
—Stephen Hawking

Who is someone around you who doesn't talk much? That doesn't mean there's not a lot going on in their head. Today, seek this person out. Find out what s/he is thinking and why.

Notes

_____

_____

_____

_____

_____

APRIL

19

*"Cats seem to go on the principle that it
never does any harm to ask for what you want."*
—Joseph Wood Krutch

What is something you want to happen? Something you need or deserve?
Instead of waiting for someone to initiate on your behalf and give it to you, how
will you ask for it?

Notes

_____

_____

_____

_____

_____

APRIL

20

"If you ask people, 'What is your passion?,' they often freeze. They feel as if they have to give an amazing answer like 'Feed the world's orphans.'"
—*Dan Pink*

What is your passion? What is a something that is calling you? And it doesn't have to be amazing.

Notes

_____

_____

_____

_____

_____

APRIL

21

"A new friend is a smile and
a good question away."
—Andrew Horn

Do you consider yourself shy? Shyness is a label that can serve as an excuse for not meeting people. Today, reach out to someone you don't know. Smile and ask for their advice–whether it's for a good place for lunch or how to finish a project.

Notes

APRIL

22

*"And the trouble is, if you don't risk
anything, you risk even more."*
—*Erica Jong*

What is something you want in your life now – but for some reason, haven't
asked for it? What is holding you back? Remind yourself, if you don't ask, the
answer is always NO.

Notes

_____

_____

_____

_____

_____

APRIL

23

"A year from now, you will wish
you had started today."
—Karen Lamb

What is something you've been putting off because it will "take so much time."
The longer you wait, the longer it will take. Start today… and a year from now,
you'll be glad you did.

Notes

_____

_____

_____

_____

_____

APRIL

24

"Time is a created thing. To say 'I don't have time'
is like saying 'I don't want to.'"
—*Lao Tzu*

What is something you've been saying you don't "have time" to do, but in your
heart, you know it's a regret waiting to happen? Prevent that regret. Do it...now.

Notes

_____

_____

_____

_____

_____

APRIL

25

"Dream long, plan short."
—Sheryl Sandberg

Hmm. What is something you want to experience or achieve by the end of the year? That's your long dream. Now what will you do THIS WEEK to set it in motion? That's your short plan.

Notes

_____

_____

_____

_____

_____

APRIL

26

"The world needs dreamers and the world needs doers. But above all, the world needs dreamers who do."
—Sarah Ban Breathnach

What is your dream? What are you doing to make it come true? What are two things you will do this week to move it forward, to make it a reality?

Notes

_____

_____

_____

_____

_____

APRIL

27

*"A glorious thing when one has not
unlearned what it means to begin."*
—Martin Buber

Today, I will begin to _____.

Notes

_____

_____

_____

_____

_____

APRIL

28

"Success is not about wealth, fame or power, but how many shining eyes I have around me."
—Ben Zander

Who is someone around you who has shining eyes? How will you thank them for their light?

Notes

_____

_____

_____

_____

_____

APRIL

29

*"There are always two voices sounding in
our ears – the voice of fear and the voice of confidence.
One is the clamor of the senses,
the other is the whispering of the higher self."*
—*Charles Newcomb*

What is something you want to try? Which voice are you listening to?

Notes

_____

_____

_____

_____

_____

APRIL

30

*"When you're surrounded by people who
share a passionate commitment around a
common purpose, anything is possible."*
—*Howard Schultz*

Think back to a time you were surrounded by people who shared a passionate commitment around a common purpose. What was that situation? Were you a part of an athletic team? A choir or band? A fund- raising initiative? A political campaign? Describe what it was like to be part of that group.

Notes

_____

_____

_____

_____

_____

*"The most important
things in the world
aren't things."*

—Ann Landers

MAY

I GREW UP IN A small town in Southern California. More horses than people. Our family of five lived on my dad's salary as a high school teacher.

I'll always remember one particular Christmas, our mom told us we couldn't afford the things our friends were getting that we had asked for.

We were unhappy about it at the time and she shared Ann Landers' quote with us.

I didn't appreciate that advice at the time, but have grown to believe this is one of life's profound truths.

How about you? Have you been wanting some things–a new house, a bigger car, household items, or clothes–and you're disappointed because you can't afford them?

Does remembering Ann Landers' quote put things in perspective and remind you that you may already be wealthy in what matters?

MAY

1

"Meaning makes us happy, not money.
And everyone can afford that."
—Sam Horn

When will we understand that money is important, but it's not the Holy Grail of Happiness? I bet you know someone who has lots of money, but they're still unhappy. What are three things that give your life meaning? Do you understand you're already wealthy in what matters?

Notes

_____

_____

_____

_____

_____

MAY

2

"Time is the new money."
—Richard Branson

What does this quote mean to you? If time is money, are you spending it wisely?

Notes

_____

_____

_____

_____

_____

MAY

3

"Money can't buy me love."
—Paul McCartney

Who is someone you love? What will you do today – that doesn't cost any money–to show them how much they mean to you? Send a letter? Take time to call? Clean their home or yard?

Notes

_____

_____

_____

_____

_____

MAY

4

"You're not wealthy until you have something money can't buy."
—*Garth Brooks*

How are you wealthy in what money can't buy?

Notes

_____

_____

_____

_____

_____

MAY

5

"Children spell love differently.
They spell it T-I-M-E."
—sign in doctor's office

I remember seeing this sign in our paediatrician's office. It reminded me that my presence was far more important than any presents I could give my sons. Today, give someone you love the gift of your undivided attention and time.

Notes

_____

_____

_____

_____

_____

MAY

6

"I wish everyone could be rich and famous so they would know for themselves it's not the answer."
—*Jim Carrey*

Have you seen the studies of lottery winners that say many "wish it had never happened"? You may think, "I'd like to give it a try anyway." The point is, fame and fortune don't guarantee happiness. What are three things that enrich your life that don't cost a penny?

Notes

_____

_____

_____

_____

_____

MAY

7

"Not everything that can be counted counts, and not
everything that counts can be counted."
—Albert Einstein

Einstein was right. The Hedonic Treadmill is a psychological phenomenon that states we pursue pleasurable things—wealth, status, stuff – in the mistaken belief they'll make us happy. When we finally achieve or acquire them, they're nice for a while, but we quickly get accustomed to them.

Since they're no longer satisfying, we seek more, in a never-ceasing search for contentment. That perpetual cycle produces "never have enough, never feel we're enough"emptiness.

Notes

_____

_____

_____

_____

_____

MAY

8

"Writing is the only thing that when I do it, I don't feel I should be doing something else."
—Gloria Steinem

What do you do – that when you do it – you don't want to be doing anything else? Playing music? A hobby or sport? Games? How will you make time for that today?

Notes

_____

_____

_____

_____

_____

MAY

9

*"The moment one gives close attention to anything,
even a blade of grass, it becomes an indescribable
source of wonder and beauty."*
—Henry Miller

Today, give close attention to a flower, to a painting or piece of art, to someone you love. In seconds, it can become an indescribable source of wonder and beauty.

Notes

_____

_____

_____

_____

_____

MAY

10

"The intuitive mind is a sacred gift and the rational mind is a faithful servant. We have created a society that honors the servant and has forgotten the gift."
—Albert Einstein

Do you consider only logic – use only your rational mind–when making a decision? Today, tap into your emotions – your gut and intuition – and ask yourself what they're telling you.

Notes

_____

_____

_____

_____

_____

MAY

11

"My mother told me to be a lady. And for her that meant be your own person, be independent."
—*Ruth Bader Ginsberg*

What advice did your parents give you? What is something they told you that has stuck with you? How has it impacted your life?

Notes

_____

_____

_____

_____

_____

MAY

12

"Life doesn't come with a manual,
it comes with a mother."
—Mother's Day card

I'll always remember my teen-aged sons giving me this card. It was a much-welcomed vote of confidence that at least part of what I was saying was getting through. What was something your mother said or did that has had lasting impact on you? What was she a manual for?

Notes

_____

_____

_____

_____

_____

MAY

13

"Each morning we are born again.
What we do today is what matters most."
—*Buddha*

Give yourself a fresh start. Instead of regretting something that happened in the past, or thinking ahead to this weekend, focus on what you could do TODAY that would really matter.

Notes

_____

_____

_____

_____

_____

MAY

14

*"Do something today your future
self will thank you for."*
—*sign in gym*

Look ahead to the end of this month. What would your future self thank you
for starting, stopping, or doing differently? Jot it down, then check back on May
31 to gauge your progress.

Notes

_____

_____

_____

_____

_____

MAY

15

"You can't have everything.
Where would you put it?"
—George Carlin

Look around your home. Do you have a lot of "stuff?" Does it feel messy, cluttered? Or is there a place for everything and everything is in its place?

Notes

_____

_____

_____

_____

_____

MAY

16

*"In the scope of a happy life, a messy
desk or overstuffed closet may seem trivial,
yet I find getting rid of clutter gives a disproportionate
boost to happiness."*
—Gretchen Rubin

Get rid of one piece of clutter everyday. Put two garbage bags out- one for items to donate, one for items to throwaway. When you pick something up, it either goes back where it belongs because it's beautiful, functional or meaningful or it goes in one of the other bags.

Notes

_____

_____

_____

_____

_____

MAY

17

"After one has been in prison, it is the
small things one appreciates, like being able to take
a walk whenever one wants. The simple act of being
able to control one's person."
—Nelson Mandela

Are there aspects of your life you don't like but they're out of your control? The question is, what is in your control? Bringing ONE thing into your life that puts the light on in your eyes can compensate for the other 95% that is out of your control.

Notes

_____

_____

_____

_____

MAY

18

"If you have to buy more stuff to store your stuff,
maybe you have too much stuff."
—George Carlin

Do you have too much stuff? As the saying goes, "First we own our possessions, then they own us."
 Do you have
a) not enough possessions,
b) too many possessions,
c) just the right amount and type of possessions?

Notes

_____

_____

_____

_____

_____

MAY

19

"You'd have a lot more followers if you acted like you only needed ten."
—*Josh Spector*

If you're on social media, you probably "get" what Josh Spector is talking about. There's a certain desperateness that comes across when it's clear someone is chasing "clicks." When you think about it, the same insight applies when you substitute the word "friends" for followers."

Hmmm. Discuss.

Notes

_____

_____

_____

_____

_____

MAY

20

*"Of all the things that truly matter, getting more
things done is not one of them."*
—Mike Dooley

Somewhere along the line many of us got the message that fun is something we do only when our work is done. Since, for many of us, our work is never done, that leaves no time for fun. What is your philosophy about work and fun?

Notes

_____

_____

_____

_____

_____

MAY

21

*"Never underestimate the importance
of having fun. I am going to have fun everyday I have
left. You have to decide whether you're a Tigger or an
Eeyore."*
—*Randy Pausch*

Play dates aren't just for kids. Do something today you enjoy and that makes
you smile or laugh.

Notes

_____

_____

_____

_____

_____

MAY

22

"Until one has loved an animal, a part of one's soul remains un-awakened."
—Anatole France

Have you loved an animal? Was it a family dog? A cat who keeps you company? A horse that taught you about cooperation vs. control? What did that animal awaken in you?

Notes

_____

_____

_____

_____

_____

MAY

23

*"Attention is the rarest and purest
form of generosity."*
—Simone Weil

When you give someone your total attention, you are saying, "You are the most important thing in my world right now. Instead of thinking about anything else, I am focusing fully on you. "Who will you gift your generous attention to today?

Notes

_____

_____

_____

_____

MAY

24

"Feeling grumpy? Get out your gratitude training
wheels and ride into a good mood."
—Anne Lamott

What will you do right now to ride into a good mood?

Notes

_____

_____

_____

_____

_____

MAY

25

"The internet is just a world passing
around notes in a classroom."
—*Jon Stewart*

How much time a day do you spend online comparing yourself to others' social media posts? Is that causing you to feel "less than?" What's a healthier way to spend time on the internet?

Notes

_____

_____

_____

_____

_____

MAY

26

"Count your age by friends, not years. Count your life by smiles, not tears."
—*John Lennon*

Today, follow John Lennon's advice and count your friends. Write down the names of people who are your cheerleaders, companions, encouragers, allies. Look at how lucky you are.

Notes

_____

_____

_____

_____

_____

MAY

27

"Music is a moral law. It gives soul to the universe, wings to the mind, flight to the imagination, and charm to life."
—*Plato*

What role has music played in your life? Do you play an instrument? Attend concerts? Listen to your favorite artist on radio or iTunes? How has music contributed charm to your life?

Notes

_____

_____

_____

_____

_____

MAY

28

"Stop looking at me in that tone of voice."
—Dane Cook

A divorce attorney told me a major cause of conflict in marriage is "that look. "You know, the eye-rolling look of contempt. Are you looking at a loved one with that tone of voice? Could you be more mindful and choose to look at them with compassion instead of contempt?

Notes

_____

_____

_____

_____

_____

MAY

29

"Let us always be open to the miracle
of a second chance."
—Rev. David Steir

Has a relationship with someone you once cared for soured? Were feelings hurt? Words said? It's not too late to reach out to that person and ask for a fresh start, a second chance.

Notes

_____

_____

_____

_____

_____

MAY

30

*"What a wonderful life I've lived.
I only wish I'd realized it sooner."*
—*Colette*

Today, reflect on the life you've led. What's wonderful about it? Pinpoint at least ten blessings you've had, individuals and opportunities you're grateful for. Write them down to imprint them.

Notes

_____

_____

_____

_____

_____

MAY

31

"The clock ticks both ways!"
—Rita Dove

Please look back at what you wrote on May14. Did you do something your
future self would thank you for. What was it?

Notes

_____

_____

_____

_____

_____

"Perhaps the truth depends on a walk around the lake."

—*Wallace Stevens*

JUNE

I HAVE NEVER REGRETTED GOING for a walk. Never. Not once. How about you?

June is a wonderful month for being outside, and walking can be a rewarding form of contemplative movement.

Cheryl Strayed, author of the book WILD, says her mother used to say something that drove her nuts:

"There is a sunrise and a sunset every day and you can choose to be there for it. You can put yourself in the way of beauty."

Promise yourself you'll get up and go for a walk at sunrise this month. No phone. No distractions.

Put yourself in the way of beauty.

JUNE

"In every walk in Nature,
one receives more than he seeks."
—John Muir

Where is your favorite place in Nature? A seashore? A nearby mountain or forest trail? A river valley? Describe how you feel, what you receive when you're in Nature.

Notes

_____

_____

_____

_____

_____

JUNE

2

"Stay close to nature, it will never let you down."
—*Frank Lloyd Wright*

Feeling down? Get out in nature and look up. Instant perspective.

Notes

_____

_____

_____

_____

_____

JUNE

3

*"If in doubt, walk until your
day becomes interesting."*
—Rolf Potts

If you need to make an important decision, don't sleep on it, walk on it. Angels whisper to us when we walk.

Notes

_____

_____

_____

_____

_____

JUNE

4

"In the name of God, stop a moment,
cease your work, look around you."
—*Leo Tolstoy*

Are you rushing from the moment you get up to the moment you go to bed?
Look around and really see something or someone as if for the first time. It will
fill you with new found gratitude.

Notes

_____

_____

_____

_____

_____

JUNE

5

"The whole of life lies in the verb 'seeing.'"
—Teilhard de Chardin

Every time I see this quote, something in me says, "Yes, a thousand times yes." Three different times today, take the time to stop and really SEE what is around you. Really seeing can transform an ordinary moment into an extraordinary moment.

Notes

_____

_____

_____

_____

_____

JUNE

6

"Everything works better if you unplug it
for a few minutes. Including you."
—*Anne Lamott*

None of us will look back at the end of our life and say, "I wish I had spent more time with my head buried in my digital device." Today, set aside your phone at the dinner table. Unplug your laptop instead of taking it to bed with you.

Notes

_____

_____

_____

_____

_____

JUNE

7

*"Walk as if you are kissing the earth
with your feet."*
—*Thich Nhat Hanh*

Power-walking is a great way to get your heart-rate up. But there's something to be said for strolling. Today, walk as if your feet are kissing the earth. It will get your spirits up.

Notes

_____

_____

_____

_____

_____

JUNE

"You have brains in your head.
You have feet in your shoes. You can steer
yourself in any direction you choose."
—Dr. Seuss

Are you satisfied with the current direction of your life, career or relationship? If not, what new or different direction will you choose?

Notes

_____

_____

_____

_____

_____

JUNE

"Truly wonderful the mind of a child is."
—Yoda in Star Wars

It's impossible to be jaded when around a curious child. Watch them explore and be delighted at the simplest things. Today, how could you be more child-like in how you view the world?

Notes

_____

_____

_____

_____

_____

JUNE

10

"If there were a rehab for curiosity,
I'd be in it."
—Diane Sawyer

Would you say you are a curious person? What is an example of that?

Notes

_____

_____

_____

_____

_____

JUNE

11

"It is always with excitement that I wake up in the morning wondering what my intuition will toss up to me, like gifts from the sea. I work with it and rely on it. It's my partner."
—Jonas Salk

Sometimes, our life can get so busy, we don't have time to listen to the gifts out intuition tosses to us. What could you do to change that?

Notes

_____

_____

_____

_____

_____

JUNE

12

"I told the doctor I couldn't relax.
He said, 'Force yourself.'"
—Len Dettinger

I ended up in Urgent Care because I "soldiered through" a serious respiratory ailment for weeks. The doctor said, "If you don't take better care of yourself, your body will do something more drastic to get your attention." Are you going, going, going? At what cost? How can you force yourself to relax?

Notes

_____

_____

_____

_____

_____

JUNE

13

"Drag your thoughts away from your troubles—by the ears, by the heels, anyway you can manage it. It's the healthiest thing a body can do."
—Mark Twain

We can't drag our mind away from troubling thoughts by trying to STOP them. The more we say, "I am NOT going to worry, "the more we worry. Instead, replace troubling thoughts with what we DO want, "I trust she is safe. I am confident this will workout for the best."

Notes

_____

_____

_____

_____

_____

JUNE

14

"Some people have analysis. I have Utah."
—Robert Redford

Where is your Utah? The science of Ergonomics says your home is your First Place and your job is your Second Place. Your Third Place; (e.g., a library, park, bookstore or coffee shop) is a nurturing place where you can be your "true self." Where do you go to nourish yourself?

Notes

_____

_____

_____

_____

_____

JUNE

15

"I believe the greatest gift you can give the family and the world is a healthy you."
—*Joyce Meyers*

Do you agree with Joyce Meyers? Are you giving your family and the world a healthy you–or are you neglecting your health? What is one thing you can do today to contribute to a healthier you?

Notes

_____

_____

_____

_____

_____

JUNE

16

*"My father gave me the greatest gift
anyone could give another person—he
believed in me."*
—Jim Valvano

Did your father believe in you? How so? Have you thanked him for it? If he's
gone, can you pass on what he did for you to someone else to pay it forward?
And if your father didn't believe in you, who did? Reach out today to say,
"Thank you."

Notes

_____

_____

_____

_____

_____

JUNE

17

"We are all just walking each other home."
—*Ram Dass*

Who are you walking side-by-side with? Who are you walking home?

Notes

_____

_____

_____

_____

_____

JUNE

18

"To me, life boils down to one thing, it's movement."
—Jerry Seinfeld

Today, get a move on. Sitting is the new cigarettes. Get up out of that chair or off that sofa. Get outside and get moving.

Notes

_____

_____

_____

_____

_____

JUNE

19

"Action is the antidote to despair."
—Joan Baez

Feeling discouraged? What action can you take to feel better about yourself and your life?

Notes

_____

_____

_____

_____

_____

JUNE

20

"I want adventure in the great wide somewhere."
—Belle from Beauty in the Beast

What's an adventure that's calling you? Something new and different that would challenge you? That would put the light on in your eyes? Write it down here and describe it in detail.

Notes

_____

_____

_____

_____

_____

JUNE

21

"If at the end of the day I can say I've had fun,
it was a good day."
—Simone Biles

Champion athletes know we set up flow when we're having fun. It's not indulgent, its an investment in improved performance. What will you do to set up fun and flow today?

Notes

_____

_____

_____

_____

_____

JUNE

22

*"Self-discipline is the ability to make
yourself do something you don't necessarily want to do,
to get a result you would really like to have."*
—Andy Andrews

My son has a different way of saying this. When it comes to exercising and eating right, Andrew says, "Discipline is remembering what you want. "What do you want? Today, how will you focus on the result you want to receive instead of the reason you don't feel like doing it?

Notes

_____

_____

_____

_____

_____

JUNE

23

"Sweat is fat crying."
—sign in gym

Don't you always feel better after you've worked out? It really does flush toxins – physical and emotional – out of your system. Today, build up your self-esteem by building up a good sweat.

Notes

_____

_____

_____

_____

_____

JUNE

24

*"It is an old and ironic habit of human beings to run
faster when we have lost our way."*
—Rollo May

Do you ever feel the hurrieder you go, the behinder you get? Today, could you
slow down and be more present to how you go about your day? No rushing, just
mindful movement.

Notes

_____

_____

_____

_____

_____

JUNE

25

*"We are here and it is now. Further than that, all
human knowledge is moonshine."*
—H. L. Mencken

Are you getting ahead of yourself? Fretting about the future doesn't help.
Instead, take a big deep breath RIGHT NOW and be here, be now. It is the
ultimate wisdom.

Notes

_____

_____

_____

_____

_____

JUNE

26

"The first step towards getting somewhere is to decide you're not going to STAY where you are."
—*J. P. Morgan*

Can you believe it? The year is half over. Please look back to the beginning of this year. Have you made progress? How so? What is an area of your life you're NOT content to stay where you are?

Notes

_____

_____

_____

_____

_____

JUNE

27

"When was the last time you looked at the stars with the wonder they deserved?"
—*Kris Kristofferson*

When my sons went off to college, I sat them down for 'da talk. You know the one I mean. Where we try to distill everything we've learned about life into a few pieces of advice. One was, "If you ever feel discouraged, get outside and look up. It's hard to feel down when you're looking up."

Notes

_____

_____

_____

_____

_____

JUNE

28

"I'm not a loner, I'm an ambivert."
—Sam Horn

Introverts are energized by solitude. Extroverts are energized by socialization. Ambiverts are energized by a mix of both. Which are you? Why do you think that?

Notes

_____

_____

_____

_____

_____

JUNE

29

*"The most common way people give up their power is
to think they don't have any."*
—Alice Walker

Power is simply "the ability to get things done." Do you feel powerful? Why
or why not?

Notes

_____

_____

_____

_____

_____

JUNE

30

*"Consult not your fears, but your hopes
and dreams. Think not about your frustrations,
but about your unfulfilled potential."*
—*Pope John XXIII*

Is there an area of your life that's not what you want it to be? Instead of consulting your fears or frustrations, could you instead consult your hopes and dreams? What does that look/sound like?

Notes

_____

_____

_____

_____

_____

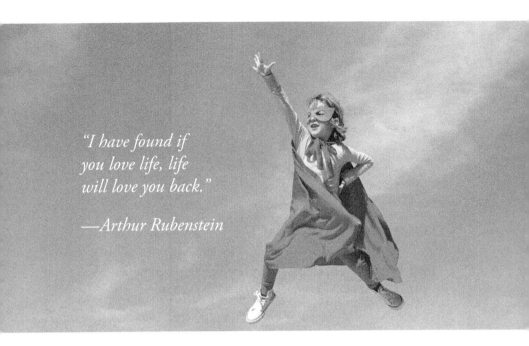

"I have found if you love life, life will love you back."

—Arthur Rubenstein

JULY

ARTHUR RUBENSTEIN WAS RIGHT. We've got to go first. Whatever we want other people to feel, we've got to feel first. Our attitude sets the precedent.

This month, choose words that produce what you do want instead of what you don't.

Instead of saying, "I'm dreading Monday," say, "I'm looking forward to Monday."

Instead of saying, "I'm bored," say, "I'm grateful for my life." Watch what happens when you choose to love your life.

JULY

1

*"We can't learn anything from
experiences we're not having."*
—Louis L'Amour

What's an experience you had that you were initially reluctant to do? In retrospect, are you glad you tried something new? What did you learn?

Notes

_____

_____

_____

_____

_____

JULY

2

"To play it safe is not to play."
—*Robert Altman*

Are you playing it safe in a relationship, in your career, in your life? Why? At what cost? What could you do today to play full out?

Notes

_____

_____

_____

_____

_____

JULY

3

"Thinking 'Here goes nothing'
could be the start of everything."
—Drew Wagner

Perfectionism is just another word for procrastinating. What have you been putting off because you "don't have all your ducks in a row?" Could you instead say "Here's goes nothing?"

Notes

_____

_____

_____

_____

_____

JULY

*"It's far better to dare mighty things
...than to live in a gray twilight."*
—Theodore Roosevelt

Was there a time in your life you "lived in a gray twilight?" What was the situation? How did you get out of it? Did you "dare mighty things?" How so?

Notes

_____

_____

_____

_____

_____

JULY

5

"I believe life loves the lover of it."
—Maya Angelou

Start a new ritual today. Every morning, before you roll out of bed, say out loud, "I love my life, I love my life, I love my life. "You will be amazed at how it helps you start the day in a good mood.

Notes

_____

_____

_____

_____

_____

JULY

6

"When you have to make a decision and don't know
what to do, take the bolder of the options."
—*Warren Reed*

Are you facing an important decision? Not sure what to do? Take the bolder of
the options.

Notes

_____

_____

_____

_____

_____

JULY

7

*"Life expands or contracts
in proportion to our courage."*
—Anais Nin

Would you call yourself courageous? Why or why not?

Notes

_____

_____

_____

_____

_____

JULY

8

*"Once you've done the mental work,
there comes a point you have to throw yourself into
action and put your heart on the line."*
—*Phil Jackson*

When is a time you put your heart on the line?

Notes

_____

_____

_____

_____

_____

JULY

9

*"Do you see the world as a dangerous
place or as an adventurous place?"*
—*Sam Horn*

Did you grow up with adults telling you to "Be careful?" How did that
impact you?

Notes

_____

_____

_____

_____

_____

JULY

10

*"If you're brave enough to say good-bye, life will
reward you with a new hello."*
—*Paulo Coelho*

Think of a time when you were brave enough to say goodbye to something toxic-
whether it was a relationship, a job, habit, or living situation. Did something
good move into your life as a result? Something that, may not have happened
otherwise? What did you learn from that situation?

Notes

_____

_____

_____

_____

_____

JULY

11

*"We must all make the choice between
what is right and what is easy."*
—*J. K. Rowland*

When is a time you did the right thing – even when it wasn't easy?

Notes

_____

_____

_____

_____

_____

JULY

12

*"If you don't think you're worthy,
you're never going to make it."*
—*Misty Copeland*

Ballerina Misty Copeland overcame seemingly impossible odds because she kept telling herself she was worthy. How about you? Deep down, do you feel you're worthy? Why or why not?

Notes

_____

_____

_____

_____

_____

JULY

13

*"I don't like to gamble, but I'm
willing to bet on myself."*
—Beyonce

When was a time you gambled on yourself? A time you believed in yourself and
bet on yourself?

Notes

_____

_____

_____

_____

_____

JULY

14

*"People are always looking for the single
magic bullet that will totally change everything. There
is no single magic bullet."*
—*Temple Grandin*

Temple's right. There is no magic bullet. But small changes can have a big impact. What is one thing you will change today to like yourself and your life a bit better?

Notes

_____

_____

_____

_____

_____

JULY

15

"I know I'm not going to get what I want,
so I'm not going to get my hopes up."
—*overheard in a restaurant*

Yikes. Do you know someone who's given up hope? What advice would you like
to give them?

Notes

_____

_____

_____

_____

_____

JULY

16

*"Creativity is based on the belief that
there's no particular virtue in doing things the way
they've always been done."*
—Rudolph Flesch

What is something you always do the same way? How can you "do the new" today?

Notes

_____

_____

_____

_____

_____

JULY

17

*"A lot of what we ascribe to luck isn't luck at all.
It's seizing the opportunity and accepting responsibility
for your future."*
—Howard Schultz, founder of Starbucks

Do you consider yourself a "lucky" person? Why or why not?

Notes

_____

_____

_____

_____

_____

JULY

18

"Guard your good mood."
—Meryl Streep

Do you have a nay-sayer in your life who enjoys raining on your parade? Do not let that person steal your good mood. Shine on.

Notes

_____

_____

_____

_____

_____

JULY

19

*"If prayer is you talking to God,
intuition is God talking to you."*
—*Wayne Dyer*

When is a time you didn't listen to you intuition – and you wish you had?

Notes

_____

_____

_____

_____

_____

JULY

20

*"It takes courage to grow up and
be who you really are."*
—e.e. cummings

You may also be familiar with the e.e. cummings quote, "To be nobody but
yourself – in a world which is doing its best, night and day, to make you everybody else – means to fight the hardest battle which any human being can fight."
Is it a fight to be yourself? How so?

Notes

_____

_____

_____

_____

_____

JULY

21

*"You can fail at what you don't want,
so you might as well take a chance
on doing what you love."*
—*Jim Carrey*

Are you taking a chance on what you love? How so? If not, why not?

Notes

_____

_____

_____

_____

_____

JULY

22

"Are you doing what you're doing today
because it works and you want to, or because it's what
you were doing yesterday?"
—Dr. Phil McGraw

Look at your behaviors today. Are you doing them because it's the way you've always done them? How's that working for you? What's one you want to change?

Notes

_____

_____

_____

_____

_____

JULY

23

"Stop trying to make everyone happy.
You're not chocolate."
—sign in chocolate shop

Are you a people-pleaser? At what cost? Today, if you find yourself trying to please someone, could you back off and let them take responsibility for their own happiness?

Notes

_____

_____

_____

_____

_____

JULY

24

"There is no such thing as an ordinary day."
—Dan Millman

Dan says this is the most important lesson he's learned about life. How about you? Are you taking your days for granted? Today, revel in the gift of an "ordinary" day.

Notes

_____

_____

_____

_____

_____

JULY

25

"Do you remember who you were
before the world told you who you should be?"
—Charles Bukowski

What did you want to be when you were growing up? An astronaut? Artist? Professional athlete? Were you told to "get your head out of the clouds" and get serious about a "real career?" Who were you – before the world told you what you could or should be?

Notes

_____

_____

_____

_____

_____

JULY

26

"You may be disappointed if you fail,
but you are doomed if you don't try."
—Beverly Sills

What is something you want to try, but you're afraid it might fail? Remind yourself that the failure is not trying.

Notes

_____

_____

_____

_____

_____

JULY

27

*"Everything can be taken from a man but one
thing—the last of the human freedoms, to choose one's
attitude in any given set of circumstances."*
—Victor Frankl

You may not be able to control your circumstances, you can control your attitude. How will you change the way you're thinking about something in your life that's not to your liking?

Notes

_____

_____

_____

_____

_____

JULY

28

"Do the best you can until you know better.
When you know better, do better."
—Maya Angelou

Are you tempted to quit an activity because you're not THE best? The question is, are you doing YOUR best? Quitting won't help you get better.

Notes

_____

_____

_____

_____

_____

JULY

29

*"Some of us are not living our dreams
because we're living our fears."*
—Les Brown

Who is someone you know who is not living their dreams because they're living
their fears? What advice would you like to give them?

Notes

_____

_____

_____

_____

_____

JULY

30

"Courage is a love affair with the unknown."
—Osho

Some people are afraid of the unknown. How about you? Do you welcome it or avoid it?

Notes

_____

_____

_____

_____

_____

JULY

31

*"There's no wiggle room when it
comes to taking responsibility for your life.
You either do it or you don't."*
—Joyce Meyers

My son's high school teacher got tired of hearing students blame and complain. She put Joyce Meyers' quote up in her classroom. When students gave her an excuse for something that went wrong, she'd just point to the quote and say, "Even if it's not your fault, it is your responsibility to fix it." Your thoughts?

Notes

_____

_____

_____

_____

_____

AUGUST

"The purpose of life is not to be happy – but to matter, to be productive, useful, to have it make some difference that you have lived at all."
—*Leo Rosten*

I'LL ALWAYS BE GRATEFUL to a college philosophy professor who told our class it wasn't enough to study Plato, Socrates and Aristotle.

He believed it was important for each of us to craft a less-than-fifty-word mission statement articulating our purpose so we had a clear "North Star" guiding our actions.

I developed mine based on Leo Rosten's quote.

"My purpose is to make a positive difference for as many people as possible, while maintaining a happy, healthy, grateful life with family and friends."

How about you? Can you state your purpose in one sentence? Do you have a less than-50-word mission statement that serves as a "North Star" to guide your actions?

If so, good for you. If not, take the time to craft one. You'll be glad you did.

AUGUST

1

"Here's a test to find out whether your mission in life is complete. If you're alive, it isn't."
—*Lauren Bacall*

Can you state your mission in life in one sentence? If you can, good for you. If you can't, craft one today. Keep coming back to this page and tweaking it until you wouldn't change a word. That mission will serve as your "North Star"and guide your actions on a daily basis.

Notes

_____

_____

_____

_____

_____

AUGUST

2

"I want to put a ding in the universe."
—Steve Jobs

How have you already made a difference – put a ding in the universe?

Notes

_____

_____

_____

_____

_____

AUGUST

3

"I learned that having nothing
but fun wasn't all that much fun."
—*Michael Phelps*

This is the epiphany Michael Phelps had when he quit swimming after the Olympics and "partied hearty." He decided to re-dedicate himself to swimming because it gave his life purpose and meaning. How about you? What gives your life purpose and meaning?

Notes

_____

_____

_____

_____

_____

AUGUST

"I alone cannot change the world,
but I can cast a stone across the waters
to create many ripples."
—Mother Teresa

Who is someone at work or in your community who has "cast a stone across the waters and created many positive ripples?" What did they do?

Notes

_____

_____

_____

_____

_____

AUGUST

5

"If you're feeling helpless, go help someone."
—Aung San Suu Kyi

Nobel Peace Prize winner Aung San Suu Kyi is right. The quickest way
to reverse a feeling of helplessness is to help someone. Who will you help
today? How?

Notes

_____

_____

_____

_____

_____

AUGUST

6

"Life consists of what a man is thinking all day."
—Ralph Waldo Emerson

Our greatest philosophers agree. As we think, so we are. If you start worrying or regretting today, turn those thoughts to what's right in your world. The most immediate, direct way to improve the quality of your life is to improve the quality of your thoughts.

Notes

_____

_____

_____

_____

_____

AUGUST

7

"One person can make a difference
and everyone should try."
—John F. Kennedy

Do you get discouraged by the news? Do you ever feel helpless with what's going on in the world? You can make a difference today. Reach out to someone who needs to know they're not alone. Give them the support or encouragement they need.

Notes

_____

_____

_____

_____

_____

AUGUST

*"It's hard to stay on purpose if we don't
know what our purpose is."*
—Sam Horn

Would you say you're living on purpose? If so, why so? If not, why not? If not,
what can you do today to get yourself back on purpose?

Notes

_____

_____

_____

_____

AUGUST

9

"If you don't design your own life plan, chances are you'll fall into someone else's plan. And guess what they have planned for you? Not much."
—*Jim Rohn*

Are you following your own life plan or someone else's? An orthodontist in my SOMEDAY workshop had set aside his dream of studying in astronomy because his parents told him he'd never be able to make a living at it. He had a lucrative practice but his heart wasn't in it. He realized it wasn't too late and now drives to the UC Berkeley Observatory once a week to take classes with a world-renowned astronomer. What is an abandoned dream you'd like to put your heart into?

Notes

_____

_____

_____

_____

_____

AUGUST

10

"We have to decide what kind of difference we're going to make."
—Jane Goodall

We all have the ability to make a difference on any given day. Who deserves some recognition? Reach out today to someone who is being overlooked to give them the attention and appreciation they deserve.

Notes

_____

_____

_____

_____

_____

AUGUST

11

*"Everyone thinks of changing the world, no one thinks
of changing himself."*
—*Leo Tolstoy*

What would you like to change about the world? Would you like people to stop fighting? Where in your life are you fighting with someone?

Would you like people to be kinder? How can you be kinder?

Notes

_____

_____

_____

_____

_____

AUGUST

12

*"Destiny is not a matter of chance,
it is a matter of choice, it not a thing to be waited for,
it is a thing to be achieved."*
—*William Jennings Bryan*

Are you choosing your destiny or is it choosing you? What are you here to do?
What are you doing to contribute to the legacy you want to leave… now, not
later in life?

Notes

_____

_____

_____

_____

_____

AUGUST

13

"If we're not happy here, we won't be happy there."
—Sam Horn

Yes, it's important to have a purposeful goal you're working towards, but your happiness can't be dependent on achieving that. Because that would mean your happiness is always out there somewhere, and you want it to be right here. What can you do to be happier here and now?

Notes

_____

_____

_____

_____

_____

AUGUST

14

> *"When you cease to make a contribution, you begin to die."*
> —*Eleanor Roosevelt*

Regardless of our age, we've got to feel we're making a difference or what's the point? Who is an older person in your life who may feel they're not contributing? How can you ask for their advice? How can you give them a chance to make a difference and feel they matter?

Notes

_____

_____

_____

_____

_____

AUGUST

15

*"A quilt may take a year,
but if you keep doing it, you get a quilt."*
—sign in a quilting store

Are you working on something that's taking a long time? Are you tempted to throw in the towel? Remember: if you keep working, you will have something to show for your efforts. That could give you just the incentive you need to keep on keeping on.

Notes

_____

_____

_____

_____

_____

AUGUST

16

*"If the words aren't coming, I go into
my library and look at my books and tell myself, 'I've
done it before and I can do it again.'"*
—*Dean Koontz*

Are you doubting yourself? Are the results not coming? Can you go into your library of memories, think of a time you succeeded and tell yourself, "I did it before, I can do it again."

Notes

_____

_____

_____

_____

_____

AUGUST

17

"Our happiness is in our hands."
—Sam Horn

A quick way to boost your spirits is to do something hands-on. Margaret Thatcher was asked her most satisfying achievement in her first year as Prime Minister. She said, "Helping my daughter paint her house." What is something tangible you can do today to have "hands-on happiness?"

Notes

_____

_____

_____

_____

AUGUST

18

"Argue for your limitations,
and sure enough, they're yours."
—Richard Bach

Are you talking yourself INTO an opportunity or OUT of it?

Notes

_____

_____

_____

_____

_____

AUGUST

19

*"The travel impulse is mental passion
and a physical curiosity. I can't understand people
who don't want to travel."*
—Paul Thoreaux

Do you have an impulse to travel? Where? When?

Notes

_____

_____

_____

_____

_____

AUGUST

20

"Believe in yourself.
Even if you don't, pretend you do,
and at some point, you will."
—Venus Williams

This was the advice Venus gave when asked the secret to being a winner. Do you feel like you're a winner? If so, why so. If not, why not?

Notes

_____

_____

_____

_____

_____

AUGUST

21

"After all, tomorrow is another day."
—Margaret Mitchell

This could be called the "Scarlet O'Hara Philosophy." Do you think this a wise approach to life? If so, why? If not, why not?

Notes

_____

_____

_____

_____

_____

AUGUST

22

"Spend your free time the way you'd like, not the way you think you're supposed to."
—*Susan Cain*

You may be thinking, "What free time?" However, if you do have free time, please understand it's supposed to be free of obligations.

Obligations are what you do with the rest of your time. Free time is for YOU. What do YOU want to do?

Notes

_____

_____

_____

_____

_____

AUGUST

23

"Where do you go to replenish yourself?
This is not a luxury. It is a necessity if you don't
want your energy to run dry. Each of us needs a little
psychic territory."
—Gloria Steinem

Remember that free time we talked about yesterday? Think of it as your psychic territory. A place you can go to replenish your energy. Where is that?

Notes

_____

_____

_____

_____

_____

AUGUST

24

"We don't want to get to the top of the ladder and find out it's against the wrong wall."
—*Thomas Merton*

Are you climbing a ladder? Is it against the right wall? If so, how so? If not, why not? What wall is it against? Is there anything you can do about it?

Notes

_____

_____

_____

_____

_____

AUGUST

25

"It's all about iteration."
—Miki Agrawal

Entrepreneurs know that "don't have to know to go." In fact, if you wait to know, you'll never go. So, what is something you've been putting off? Start... and iterate along the way.

Notes

_____

_____

_____

_____

_____

AUGUST

26

"Are you putting aside what you want
most for what you want now?"
—Zig Ziglar

Let's talk about your health. What do you want now? That bowl of ice cream? To sit on the couch and watch TV? What do you want most? To live a long, healthy life? Choose.

Notes

_____

_____

_____

_____

_____

AUGUST

27

"When we neglect what matters most to us, then that becomes the matter with us."
—*Paula Reeves*

Let's talk about health again. What is something that you're neglecting? Give it the attention and action it deserves today.

Notes

_____

_____

_____

_____

_____

AUGUST

28

"To feel, think, love and learn; surely that is being
alive and young in the real sense."
—Freya Stark

What a wonderful prescription for a well-lived day. What will you feel today?
Who will you love? What will you learn?

Notes

_____

_____

_____

_____

_____

AUGUST

29

*"I'd rather regret the things I've done than
regret the things I haven't done."*
—Lucille Ball

Do you have a regret in your life? What is it? If you could have a "do- over,"
if you knew THEN what you know NOW, how would you have handled the
situation differently?

Notes

_____

_____

_____

_____

_____

AUGUST

30

"Somewhere, something incredible
is waiting to be known."
—*Carl Sagan*

Tonight, look up at the stars. And if it's overcast, raining or snowing, imagine the stars. Tell yourself good things are coming your way, something incredible is about to happen.

Notes

_____

_____

_____

_____

_____

AUGUST

31

"Don't look at your feet to see
if you're doing it right, just dance."
—*Anne Lamott*

Today, instead of obsessing over whether you're getting it" right, "just dance. Relax. Enjoy.

Notes

_____

_____

_____

_____

_____

SEPTEMBER

"Nothing ever really goes away until it has taught us what we need to know."
—Pema Chodron

Every time I see this, I chuckle.

Why? Because it is such a reliable litmus test of whether we've learned the lesson that went with that mistake.

If this situation keeps cropping up, if this person keeps popping up, we haven't.

So, what is something you keep encountering in your life that you wish would just go away?

It won't go away until you get an AHA around it.

What is a new way to look at this? What could you do differently to get a different result? What haven't you tried yet that might just work?

SEPTEMBER

1

*"Even though you get the monkey off your back,
the circus never really leaves town."*
—Anne Lamott

A woman in a Tongue Fu! workshop said this quote described her family
perfectly. She wanted to learn how to not let her "crazy" family drive her crazy.
Do you have a "circus that never leaves town" in your life? How do you cope?

Notes

_____

_____

_____

_____

_____

SEPTEMBER

2

"If you want things to be different, perhaps the answer is to be different yourself."
—*Norman Vincent Peale*

Do three things differently today. If you always go the same way to work, take a different way. If you always have lunch at your desk, get up and go somewhere. If you always watch TV during dinner, turn it off and have a conversation. Write on this page tonight about how it felt.

Notes

_____

_____

_____

_____

_____

SEPTEMBER

3

"Self-reflection is the school of wisdom."
—*Baltasar Gracian*

It's easy to live on the surface when we're busy. We can counteract that by setting aside a few minutes for reflection before we go to sleep. What went well today? What do I want to change? How could I make tomorrow even more satisfying?

Notes

_____

_____

_____

_____

_____

SEPTEMBER

4

"Life is not fair. Get used to it."
—Bill Gates

If you understand life is unfair, it's easier to accept things that don't go your way. Does this help reframe something that happened to you that was unfair and undeserved?

Notes

_____

_____

_____

_____

_____

SEPTEMBER
5

"Life may give you a cactus.
That doesn't mean you have to sit on it."
—*Joyce Meyers*

Did something go wrong yesterday? Did something happen that wasn't right,-
fair or deserved? You can dwell on it, or you can decide what you're going to do
about it. What's it going to be?

Notes

_____

_____

_____

_____

_____

SEPTEMBER

"Quit watering dead plants."
—Sam Horn

Have you been taught that winners never quit? Sometimes it's just the opposite. Is there something toxic in your life – a dead plant? Would it be wise to stop watering it?

Notes

_____

_____

_____

_____

_____

SEPTEMBER

7

"People treat us the way we teach them to treat us."
—Jack Canfield

Is someone "taking advantage" of you? Please understand that silence sanctions. If you don't speak up, they'll conclude you don't mind because you're "not saying anything." Say something!

Notes

_____

_____

_____

_____

_____

SEPTEMBER

*"My friend thought he'd never get a date.
I told him to think positive. Now he's positive he's
never going to get a date."*
—*Brother Sammy Shore*

Have you promised yourself you'll try something new, but in your mind you're already "positive" it won't work? Change your tune if you want to succeed. Tell yourself, "Give it a chance. I don't know if I don't try."

Notes

_____

_____

_____

_____

_____

SEPTEMBER

9

"The need for change bulldozed
a road down the center of my brain."
—Maya Angelou

Actually, the need to change doesn't usually bulldoze a road down the center of our brain, it whispers, it nudges, it calls. What is a change you've been wanting to make, and it's not necessarily a big change, it's just something a tad different that feels right?

Notes

_____

_____

_____

_____

_____

SEPTEMBER

10

"If you really want to do something, you'll find a way.
If you don't; you'll find an excuse."
—*Jim Rohn*

When is a time you found a way to achieve something – even when the odds were against it? What was the situation? Describe what it felt like–how satisfying it was.

Notes

_____

_____

_____

_____

_____

SEPTEMBER

11

"Exceptions are the slippery slope of boundaries."
—Sam Horn

Have you said "No thank you," but someone is pressuring you to give in and
go along, to say "Yes … just this once?" Don't let someone nibble away at your
clarity. Exceptions to the rule… become the rule.

Notes

_____

_____

_____

_____

_____

SEPTEMBER

12

*"If you don't like what's being said,
change the conversation."*
—Don Draper, MadMen

If someone makes an unfair or untrue accusation, don't deny or defend it. You'll just end up arguing (and perhaps proving) their point. If someone says, "Women are so catty," change the conversation. For example, "I've found that women are real champions of each other. In fact…"

Notes

_____

_____

_____

_____

_____

SEPTEMBER

13

"Wallowing is sex for depressives."
—*Jeanette Winterson*

Wow, that's some quote. Is there something you're wallowing in? What are the rewards?

Notes

_____

_____

_____

_____

_____

SEPTEMBER

14

*"The light at the end of the tunnel
is not an illusion. The tunnel is."*
—coffee mug slogan

What if the tunnel you're in isn't nearly as dark or difficult as you're making it
out to be? What if you told yourself a new story about it right now?

Notes

_____

_____

_____

_____

_____

SEPTEMBER

15

"Change before you have to."
—Jack Welch

When is a time you changed something because you wanted to, not because you had to? Remember how good that felt? How did making that change impact your life?

Notes

_____

_____

_____

_____

_____

SEPTEMBER

16

"One setback is one setback;
it is not the end of the world."
—Jillian Michaels

My psychologist friend Dr. Dianne Gerard says some people tend to "cata-strophize. "If something doesn't workout as planned, they project worst case scenarios. Instead, put thinks (intentional) in perspective. Remind yourself, "This is just a setback, and I will bounce back."

Notes

_____

_____

_____

_____

_____

SEPTEMBER

17

"The mark of a successful organization isn't whether it has problems; it's whether it has the same problems it had last year."
—*John Foster Dulles*

None of us are perfect. We'll always have problems. The question is, are they the same problems we had last year? What is one thing you'll do differently today?

Notes

_____

_____

_____

_____

_____

SEPTEMBER

18

*"We should learn from them is takes of others. We
don't have time to make them all ourselves."*
—*Groucho Marx*

If someone makes a mistake today – whether it's you or someone else – don't lament it, learn from it. Ask yourself, "How could this be prevented or handled more effectively in the future?"

Notes

_____

_____

_____

_____

_____

SEPTEMBER

19

"Sometimes people try to destroy you,
precisely because they recognize your power.
Not because they don't see it, but because they see it
and don't want it to exist."
—Bell Hooks

You've heard of "Tall Poppy Syndrome?" Someone who "cuts you down to size" because they're jealous or possessive and don't want you to be bigger than them? Do you have someone in your life like that? Who is that person? What is their agenda?

Notes

_____

_____

_____

_____

_____

SEPTEMBER

20

"How do you know what's right in front of you when
you're looking the other way?"
—Anna Quindlen

On a scale of 1-10, how distracted are you? Do you have so many things competing for your attention, you rarely give any one thing your full focus? Today, really look at who and what is in front of you. Give them your eyes, your ears, your undivided attention.

Notes

_____

_____

_____

_____

_____

SEPTEMBER

21

*"Some people gets tuck simply because they're stuck
telling a story about why they're stuck."*
—*Heather Havriklesky*

What story are you telling yourself? Is it moving you forward or keeping
you stuck?

Notes

_____

_____

_____

_____

_____

SEPTEMBER

22

"The only danger is not to evolve."
—Jeff Bezos

Do you feel you've evolved in the last year? Become a better person? A better parent or partner? How so?

Notes

_____

_____

_____

_____

_____

SEPTEMBER

23

"Sometimes I lie awake at night and I ask,
'Where have I gone wrong?' Then a voice says to me,
'This is going to take more than one night.'"
—Charles M. Schulz

What a sense of humor that Charlie Brown has. Laying awake at night dwelling on what we've done wrong doesn't undo it. It's a better use of mind-time to focus on how we can fix it, learn from it, or prevent it from happening again.

Notes

_____

_____

_____

_____

_____

SEPTEMBER

24

"If your boundaries don't have metrics,
they're not boundaries."
—Sam Horn

When it comes to holding yourself accountable for changing habits, I've got one word for you. Metrics. Intentions aren't enforceable unless we attach metrics to them. What's a habit you want to change? When will you start and/or finish? What other specific numbers make this tangible?

Notes

_____

_____

_____

_____

_____

SEPTEMBER

25

"There is always a better way to do something;
find it."
—*Thomas Edison*

What is something that takes up too much of your time? How will you delegate it, pay someone else to do it, or find a better way to do it?

Notes

_____

_____

_____

_____

_____

SEPTEMBER

26

*"Some people believe holding on and
hanging in are signs of strength. However, there are
times it takes more strength to know when to
let go and then to do it."*
—*Ann Landers*

What is something you're holding on to – but the real strength is in letting it go? Say to yourself, "This experience has taught me what I need to know. Thank you, you're free to go now."

Notes

_____

_____

_____

_____

_____

SEPTEMBER

27

*"Bullies don't want a win-win; they want to win.
They put you down to keep you down so they can be
bigger than you and stay on top."*
—*Sam Horn*

Is there someone in your life and it seems like no matter what you do, you can't win? Is that person a bully – someone who doesn't want to cooperate – they want to control?

Notes

_____

_____

_____

_____

_____

SEPTEMBER

28

*"In my world, the squeaky wheel
does not get the grease."*
—Tim Gunn

Is there a squeaky wheel in your life? Instead of giving that person a lot of time and attention in the hopes of turning him/her around, why not give that time and attention to someone who is NOT causing problems, someone who is acting in integrity and deserves to be appreciated?

Notes

_____

_____

_____

_____

_____

SEPTEMBER

29

*"Did you ever wonder why
no one ever tries softer?"*
—*Lilly Tomlin*

We've been taught to work hard, to try hard. But sometimes the most meaningful experiences come easily and effortlessly. What is something in your life where you're going to try softer?

Notes

_____

_____

_____

_____

_____

SEPTEMBER

30

"If you feel your life is a see-saw, perhaps you're depending on other people for your ups and downs."
—*Sam Horn*

Do you compare yourself to other people? If so, your self-esteem will forever depend on where you are and who you're with. Instead of comparing, admire or aspire. Saying to yourself, "Good for them" or "How can I?" moves you from envy to action.

Notes

_____

_____

_____

_____

_____

OCTOBER

"The standard of success isn't the money or the stuff. It is absolutely about the amount of joy that you feel."
—Esther Hicks

WHENEVER I SEE THIS quote, something in me says, "Yes, yes, yes." Who is someone you know who is joyous?

When was the last time you experienced joy?

If you agree that one standard of success is the amount of joy you feel, what will you do this month to feel more joy?

OCTOBER

1

"Ideas are the beginning point of all fortune."
—Napoleon Hill

I'm partial to October 1 because it's the day I set out on my Year by the Water, which changed my life – for good. It all started with an idea. That ephemeral idea turned into a rewarding reality that took me around the world. What idea will you begin today to change your life – for good?

Notes

_____

_____

_____

_____

_____

OCTOBER

2

"The key to knowing joy is to be easily pleased."
—Mark Nepo

Would you say you are "easily pleased?" What is the one thing that makes you happy every time you see it or think of it?

Notes

_____

_____

_____

_____

_____

OCTOBER

3

"EUDAIMONIA means
'human flourishing, prosperity...'"
—Webster's dictionary

Would you say you're in a state of eudaimonia? If so, what is contributing to your prosperity, to you flourishing? If not, what's compromising it?

Notes

_____

_____

_____

_____

_____

OCTOBER

4

"We can only live happily-ever-after
on a day-to-day basis."
—Margaret Wander Bonnano

Don't think about how or if you're going to be happy a month or year from now. What is one thing you will do to put the light on in your eyes… today?

Notes

_____

_____

_____

_____

_____

OCTOBER

5

*"There must be more to life
than having everything."*
—Maurice Sendak

Today, count your blessings. Literally. Write down at least ten things you're thankful for, here and now.

Notes

_____

_____

_____

_____

_____

OCTOBER

6

"Money doesn't guarantee happiness;
it guarantees options."
—*Chris Rock*

Today, instead of spending money without thinking about it, ask yourself, "Is this the best use of this money? Are there better options for how I invest this?" Spend mindfully, not mindlessly.

Notes

_____

_____

_____

_____

OCTOBER

7

"Abundance is not something you acquire,
it's something you tune into."
—*Wayne Dyer*

Would you say you live an abundant life? What contributes to that? How do you
tune into it?

Notes

_____

_____

_____

_____

_____

OCTOBER

8

"I make music, you get happy. That's a good job."
—*Tommy Emmanuel*

I had the privilege of attending a sold-out concert featuring guitar legend
Tommy Emmanuel. He sad, "When I was a kid, I wanted to be in show business. Now, I just want to be in the happiness business. Agreed. When you do
your work, does it make you happy? Does it make other people happy? How so?

Notes

_____

_____

_____

_____

_____

OCTOBER

9

"Most people are about as happy
as they makeup their minds to be."
—Abraham Lincoln

Don't wait for circumstances to get better. Simply make up your mind you're going to notice what's right with your world, right here, right now.

Notes

_____

_____

_____

_____

_____

OCTOBER

10

"Joy is the best makeup."
—*Anne Lamott*

When is a time in your life you were joyful? What gives you joy now?

Notes

_____

_____

_____

_____

_____

OCTOBER

11

"Don't say maybe if you want to say no."
—Sam Horn

Do you find yourself saying yes to commitments even when you want to say no?
What's that about?

Notes

_____

_____

_____

_____

_____

OCTOBER

12

*"It is only in your thriving you have
anything to offer anyone."*
—*Esther Hicks*

Are you drained, exhausted, because you're busy taking care of others? Do you feel guilty taking time away to do something you enjoy?

Remember, it's not indulgent to do one thing every week that energizes you. It's an investment that pays off for all involved.

Notes

_____

_____

_____

_____

_____

OCTOBER

13

"The more I want to get something done,
the less I call it work."
—Richard Bach

This applies to everything–even doing chores. My mom used to put on music and gaze out the kitchen window at the field in front of our house while washing dishes. She said it was one of her favorite parts of the day. How about you? What is something that needs to get done that you might actually enjoy if you don't call it work?

Notes

_____

_____

_____

_____

_____

OCTOBER

14

*"When you are genuinely thrilled by
someone else's success, it means you are on
the right track to your own."*
—*Esther Hicks*

Who is someone you know who has experienced a recent success? A promotion?
Raise? New home? Wedding? Birth of a baby? A successful exit from their start
up? Are you genuinely happy for them? How will you reach out to give them
heartfelt congratulations?

Notes

_____

_____

_____

_____

_____

OCTOBER

15

"Why is it moral to serve the happiness of
others and not your own?"
—Ayn Rand

Is your motto, "Is everyone happy?" Do you put others first, yourself last? What is something that makes you happy? Make time for it this week. It's not selfish, it's inspiring.

Notes

_____

_____

_____

_____

_____

OCTOBER

16

"People will choose unhappiness
over uncertainty."
—*Tim Ferriss*

Do you know someone who would rather stay stuck than take a risk? Someone who would rather be unhappy than try something uncertain? If they asked for your advice, what would you say?

Notes

_____

_____

_____

_____

_____

OCTOBER

17

"When people ask, 'What is next?,'
I always say, 'THIS is next.'"
—*Fred Rogers*

I think happiness is a yin-yang balance of NOW and NEXT We are satisfied with who and where we are NOW and at the same time, we have an intriguing NEXT. What is that for you?

Notes

_____

_____

_____

_____

_____

OCTOBER

18

*"I've never scored a goal in my life without
getting a pass from someone else."*
—Abby Wambach

What a gracious observation from soccer genius Abby Wambach. How about
you? Who is someone who passed you a metaphorical ball that led to a success?
Have you thanked them?

Notes

_____

_____

_____

_____

_____

OCTOBER

19

*"It is a luxury to combine our
passion with our contribution."*
—Sheryl Sandberg

Do you see your work and recreation as separate? Do they have to be? There are ways to combine your passion with your profession. Are you already doing that? If so, kudos. If not, the next ten days share a variety of ways to do work you love that matters.

Notes

_____

_____

_____

_____

_____

OCTOBER

20

"72% of people say they are unhappy at work."
—2016 Gallup poll

There are hundreds of social media memes expressing how much people hate their job. Everything from "Sorry I was late. I was sitting in the parking lot not wanting to come in" to "I haven't gone to bed yet and I'm already looking forward to coming home from work tomorrow."

We spend a third or more of our life at work. It is not a joke to be unhappy for a third or more of our life. It is not okay to simply accept that work sucks or hope it will get better…someday. Hope is not a strategy.

On a scale of 1 – 10, how happy are you with your work?

Notes

_____

_____

_____

_____

_____

OCTOBER

21

*"Everybody is a genius. But if you judge a fish
by its ability to climb a tree, it will spend its whole life
believing it is stupid."*
—*Albert Einstein*

Do you feel you're in the wrong career, profession or industry? Do you feel like you're a fish trying to climb a tree? How so?

Notes

_____

_____

_____

_____

_____

OCTOBER

22

*"I've never seen a difference between
work and play. It's all living."*
—*Richard Branson*

Who is someone you know who sees no difference between work and play? Do you feel that's realistic or possible for you? Why or why not?

Notes

_____

_____

_____

_____

_____

OCTOBER

23

"The only way to do great work is to love what you do.
If you haven't found it yet, keep looking."
—Steve Jobs

What do you do in your free time? Noticing what you do when you're not working can reveal career options you might not have considered. What are you good at that people would either pay you to do for them, or pay you to teach to them?

Notes

_____

_____

_____

_____

_____

OCTOBER

24

"Working hard for something you don't care about is called stress. Working hard for something you love is called passion."
—Simon Sinek

What is something you're working for that you don't care about? What is something you're working hard for you love?

Notes

_____

_____

_____

_____

_____

OCTOBER

25

"Finding your passion isn't just about careers and money. It's about finding your authentic self. The one you've buried beneath other people's needs."
—*Kristen Hannah*

Would you say you've found your authentic self? Do you have rewarding work, a fulfilling career, that gives you opportunities to do what you do well? Or, did you abandon what you really wanted to do to make other people happy, to serve their needs or interests?

Notes

_____

_____

_____

_____

_____

OCTOBER

26

"Never stop questioning."
—Albert Einstein

Want to create a business wrapped around what you know that other people want to know. Start with these questions.

1.   What do people tell me I'm good at? (Please note: this may come naturally, to you so you conclude it's "no big deal;" but if people consistently compliment you on it, it could be a career!)

2.   Who in business do I admire? I look at their career and think, "I wish I could do that?"

3.   Where can I provide a shortcut to people's success by leveraging what I do well? How can I save them time and money, or make them time and money?

4.   What don't people like to do–that I actually like doing?

5.   What do I find unacceptable? I look at it and think, Somebody should do something about that? "I'm as much a somebody as anybody; I'll do something about that!"

Answering these questions can help clarify a monetizable talent or ability you have that could be at the intersection of your Interests and Income.

OCTOBER

27

*"Happiness lies in the joy of achievement
and the thrill of creative effort."*
—*Franklin D. Roosevelt*

Next time you see a craft fair, art show or farmers market, go! Ask the proprietors for their "back stories." Chances are they leveraged what they cared about into a creative effort that led to the joy of achievement. Or, as a punny friend calls it, "They turned their hobby into a jobby."

Notes

_____

_____

_____

_____

_____

OCTOBER

28

"Time is free, but it's priceless. You can't own it, but
you can use it. You can't keep it, but you can spend it.
Once you've lost it, you can never get it back."
—Harvey Mackay

How do you talk about time? Do you never have enough time? Are things a
waste of time? Are you running out of time? Always behind time? Starting
today, make friends with time. Change the way you talk about it. There's
enough time for what's important. That's a good use of time.

Notes

_____

_____

_____

_____

_____

OCTOBER

29

"To do what you love and feel that it matters,
how could anything be more fun?"
—Katherine Graham

The only thing that could be more fun is to do work we love, feel it matters and do it with people we enjoy and trust. Who do you know who gets to do that? Is it you?

Notes

_____

_____

_____

_____

_____

OCTOBER

30

*"Is not life a hundred times too short
for us to bore ourselves?"*
—*Friedrich Nietzsche*

Growing up, if I ever said I was bored, my mom would say, "You better find something to do then or I'll give you something to do." How about you? Do you ever feel bored? What could you find that would re-interest you, that would give you something to do and look forward to?

Notes

_____

_____

_____

_____

_____

OCTOBER

31

"Change can be scary.
Know what's scarier? Regrets."
—coffee mug slogan

Fill in this blank. Change is _____.
Did you say it was SCARY or HARD? How about replacing that with FUN
and WELCOME?

Notes

_____

_____

_____

_____

_____

NOVEMBER

"If the only prayer we ever said was
'Thank you,' that would be enough.
—Meister Eckhart

G IVING THANKS DOESN'T JUST have to be for Thanksgiving.

This month, when you have a meal with someone, instead of talking about traffic, politics, the weather or what's wrong in the world, why not express who and what you're grateful for and why?

It will create a "rising tide" discussion that will elevate all involved.

NOVEMBER

1

"Gratitude is not a passive response to something we have been given… and is not necessarily something that is shown after the event; it is the deep, a-priori state of attention that shows we understand and are equal to the gifted nature of life."
—David Whyte

This is one of the most eloquent definitions of gratitude I've ever seen. How will you carve out time today to give your deep attention to the gifted nature of life?

Notes

_____

_____

_____

_____

_____

NOVEMBER

2

"Feeling gratitude and not expressing it is like wrapping a present and not giving it."
—*Walt Whitman*

Who is someone you're thankful for, but you haven't told them how you feel? How will you express your gratitude to them today?

Notes

_____

_____

_____

_____

_____

NOVEMBER

3

"Be thankful for what you have, you'll end up having more. If you concentrate on what you don't have, you'll never, ever have enough."
—Oprah Winfrey

Quick. What do you think of before you go to sleep? What's wrong? Uh- oh. That means you'll get more of that. Tonight concentrate on what your thankful for, and you'll get more of that.

Notes

_____

_____

_____

_____

_____

NOVEMBER

"The soul never thinks without a mental picture."
—Aristotle

Don't just think about what you want to happen today,see it happening in your mind. Visualize a vivid mental picture. Imagine how good it will feel.

Notes

_____

_____

_____

_____

_____

NOVEMBER

5

"Just beyond yourself is where you need to be."
—David Whyte

I had the pleasure and privilege of attending a workshop with corporate poet David Whyte. This evocative insight was one of my favorites of that day. What does it mean to you? What is something calling you to be a" bit beyond" who you are right now?

Notes

_____

_____

_____

_____

_____

NOVEMBER

*"A meaningful morning practice is
the lead domino of a good day."*
—Sam Horn

What is one thing you can do each morning that makes you feel so good, so it sets the tone for the rest of the day?

Notes

_____

_____

_____

_____

_____

NOVEMBER

7

"Want your breathing to direct your
mental state instead of reflect it?"
—Sam Horn

Did you know you can reduce stress with even five minutes of belly- breathing?
Today, if you're feeling tense or uptight, breathe in five counts, and out five
counts. You can counteract "fight or flight" and access a state of flow by breathing slowly, deeply, rhythmically for five minutes.

Notes

_____

_____

_____

_____

_____

NOVEMBER

"Listen to the voice that doesn't use words."
—Rumi

Do you listen to your intuition? If so, what is something wonderful that happened because you listened to the "voice that doesn't use words?"

Notes

_____

_____

_____

_____

_____

NOVEMBER

9

*"Remember, today is the tomorrow
you worried about yesterday."*
—Dale Carnegie

Dale Carnegie's quote is eye-opening, isn't it? Makes us realize that worrying doesn't serve any good purpose. What is something you're worrying about? How will you replace that with visualizations of what you DO want to happen instead of what you DON'T?

Notes

_____

_____

_____

_____

_____

NOVEMBER

10

"In a world where you can be anything, be kind."
—*Connie Schultz*

No matter what is happening to or around us, we choose how to show up.
Today, choose to show up kind.

Notes

_____

_____

_____

_____

_____

NOVEMBER

11

"How wonderful it is that nobody need wait a single moment before beginning to improve the world."
—*Anne Frank*

I remember touring Anne Frank's house in Amsterdam where she and her family hid in a secret annex during World War II. As I walked around the cramped, dark attic, I kept marveling at the light she shared despite her circumstances. If you're in the doldrums for some reason, remember Anne Frank. If she can look on the bright side in the midst of daunting circumstances, so can we.

Notes

_____

_____

_____

_____

_____

NOVEMBER

12

"A closed mouth gathers no feet."
—Sam Horn

A Tongue Fu'ism is "It can be smarter to bite our tongue than say what's on the tip of our tongue." If you're upset and about to lash out, pause. Ask yourself if you'll regret saying this. If so, put a sock in it.

Notes

_____

_____

_____

_____

_____

NOVEMBER

13

"There are only four things we can do when we're
unhappy with a situation.
We can: avoid it, argue about it,
accept it, or alter it."
—Glenna Salsbury

So, what's a situation you're unhappy with? Are you going to avoid it, argue about it, accept it or alter it?

Notes

_____

_____

_____

_____

_____

NOVEMBER

14

"Some people strengthen their society just by being the kind of people they are."
—John Gardner

Who is someone you know who "strengthens society" because of the type of person they are?

Notes

_____

_____

_____

_____

_____

NOVEMBER

15

"If you can laugh at it, you can live with it."
—*Erma Bombeck*

I saw a very tall man in an airport wearing a t-shirt that said, "No, I'm NOT a basketball player. Are you a jockey?" What a great example of someone who decided to have fun with his height instead of being frustrated by it. Where could humor be a saving grace for you?

Notes

_____

_____

_____

_____

_____

NOVEMBER

16

*"I'm at an age where my back goes
out more often than I do."*
—Phyllis Diller

Do you have back pain? Knee pain? Neck pain? How can you address it instead of ignore it or endure it? Schedule an appointment with a chiropractor, body worker or physical therapist? Get a massage? Stretch or do yoga? What can you do to take better care of yourself?

Notes

_____

_____

_____

_____

_____

NOVEMBER

17

"I started out wanting to write great poems,
then wanting to discover true poems.
Now, I want to be the poem."
—*Mark Nepo*

What an evocative image and idea. Athletes talk about getting in the zone and "being the ball." How will you get in a state of flow today and "be the poem?"

Notes

_____

_____

_____

_____

_____

NOVEMBER

18

"If you're going to be able to look back at something and laugh about it, you might as well laugh about it now."
—*Marie Osmond*

What is something that happened while you were growing up that was frustrating at the time but funny in retrospect? Could remembering that help you get perspective on a current situation?

Notes

_____

_____

_____

_____

_____

NOVEMBER
19

"Your refrigerator tells your story."
—Sam Horn

A friend helping me de-clutter my home pointed at the refrigerator and asked, "What do you see?" Pictures of my sons. Surfing. Playing Little League. At the prom. Graduating. Guess what wasn't on the refrigerator?

Pictures of me. My refrigerator was telling quite a story, and I wasn't in it. I had taken myself out of the picture of my own life. What's on your refrigerator?

Notes

_____

_____

_____

_____

_____

NOVEMBER

20

"When you carry out acts of kindness,
you get a wonderful feeling inside. It is as though
something inside your body responds and says,
'YES, this is how I ought to feel.'"
—Rabbi Harold Kushner

Let's have a week of gratitude to celebrate that giving thanks isn't just for Thanksgiving. What is an act of kindness you will carry out today? What will you do to feel good inside and out?

Notes

_____

_____

_____

_____

NOVEMBER

21

"Make yourself a blessing to someone.
Your kind smile or pat on the back just might
pull someone back from the edge."
—Carmelia Elliott

You never know when a smile or a pat on the back will mean the world to someone in need. Keep your eyes open for someone who looks like they're going through a tough time. What could you do to let them know they're not alone, that someone cares?

Notes

_____

_____

_____

_____

_____

NOVEMBER

22

"If you want children to improve, let them hear the
nice things you say about them to others."
—*Dr. Haim Ginott*

Do you have children, grandchildren, nieces, nephews or the sons and daughters of friends? Notice something special and specific about them. Praise them to their parents – when the kids are within earshot.

Notes

_____

_____

_____

_____

_____

NOVEMBER

23

"When you drink the water, remember the well."
—Chinese proverb

Are you having a holiday meal with friends and family? If so, instead of talking about the weather, politics, sports, the traffic and what's wrong with the world, why not ask everyone to share WHO and WHAT they're grateful for and WHY. Remembering and honoring what's going well in your life will create a "rising tide" conversation that elevates all involved.

Notes

_____

_____

_____

_____

_____

NOVEMBER

24

"Happiness is, in itself, a kind of gratitude."
—Joseph Wood Krutch

Have you ever thought of it this way? That a way to say thank you for the bless-ing of your life is to be happy? Instead of getting stressed today about something petty that really won't matter in the long run, can you look around instead and say, "I am happy. Thank you for my life."

Notes

_____

_____

_____

_____

_____

NOVEMBER

25

*"The very least you can do in your life is to figure out
what you hope for…and then live inside that hope."*
—Barbara Kingsolver

What is something you hope for? Starting today, live in a "hope cocoon." From
now on, doubts will bounce off it and you will hold this vision of what you want
and live inside that hope.

Notes

_____

_____

_____

_____

_____

NOVEMBER

26

*"Perhaps we never really appreciate
anything until it is challenged."*
—Anne Morrow Lindbergh

Look around you. Are you taking someone and/or something you love for
granted? Do not wait until you lose them to appreciate them. Express or show
your gratitude for them today.

Notes

_____

_____

_____

_____

_____

NOVEMBER

27

*"A man travels the world over in search of what he
needs, and returns home to find it."*
—George Moore

What does this quote mean to you? To me, it means that we don't have to travel
to Bali, or hike the Himalayas, or stroll a beach on Maui to be happy. The
happiness we seek is right here, right now... if we're grateful for what we've got.

Notes

_____

_____

_____

_____

_____

NOVEMBER

28

*"A person who is nice to you but rude
to the waiter is not a nice person."*
—Dave Barry

Is someone around you displaying dissonance? They're nice to some people, but rude to others? They are telling you who they really are. How will you reduce the time you spend with this person, and choose to be around people who are truly kind?

Notes

_____

_____

_____

_____

_____

NOVEMBER

29

*"Too many people buy things they don't
need with money they don't have to impress
people they don't like."*
—Will Rogers

Hmm. Do you know someone like this? Next time you're about to make a big purchase, ask yourself, "Who am I buying this for – and why?"

Notes

_____

_____

_____

_____

_____

NOVEMBER

30

"I'm just trying not to be sad
about the future."
—Elon Musk

When Elon Musk was asked why he is trying to solve the world's biggest problems – transportation, energy and a back-up to Planet Earth – this is what he said. What is something you can do today to make your future something you're glad (vs. sad) about?

Notes

_____

_____

_____

_____

_____

DECEMBER

"Long days. Short years."
—Eleanor Woolf

YEARS AGO, WHILE EMCEEING the Maui Writers Conference, I helped two teachers with a book they were writing about what their students wished their parents knew.

We came up with the perfect name for their project. Long Days. Short Years.

As a mom with two kids, Eleanor's advice came in handy whenever I got frustrated or impatient with my sons. Four words. Instant perspective.

How about you? Are you a parent, teacher, coach, grandparent, partner?

Do you ever find yourself getting impatient or frustrated with the people in your life?

If so, choose to look at them with love while thinking to yourself, "Long days, short years."

Four words. Instant perspective.

DECEMBER

1

"How did it get so late so soon?"
—Dr. Seuss

It's only too late if you don't start now. What is one thing you've been putting off? How will you take action on it today so you can look back and feel proud of yourself and know you did the right thing?

Notes

_____

_____

_____

_____

_____

DECEMBER

2

"Fear is excitement with the brakes on."
—Marie Forleo

Have you ever thought of fear this way? What is something you're excited about? Are you also afraid it won't work out? Instead of letting fear stop you, why not let your excitement start you?

Notes

_____

_____

_____

_____

_____

DECEMBER

3

"Stop wearing your wish bone
where your backbone ought to be."
—Elizabeth Gilbert

Sometimes we fail to keep our resolutions because we focus on what we don't want instead of what we wish for. Change "I don't want to eat carbs" to "I will eat lean, green and protein." How will you reword your resolution to say what you DO want instead of what you DON'T?

Notes

_____

_____

_____

_____

_____

DECEMBER

"We all have time machines. Some take us back. Those are called memories. Some take us forward. Those are called dreams."
—*Audrey Niffenegger*

Use your mind as a time machine for the next four minutes. Take two minutes to think back to favorite memories. What are they? A birthday party? Vacation to Disneyland? Graduation? Now travel forward. What is something you're dreaming of? Revel in your mental time machine.

Notes

_____

_____

_____

_____

_____

DECEMBER

5

"Tears are words that need to be written."
—Paulo Coelho

Are you sad about something? Instead of holding back tears—why not write out your tears? Write out what's disappointed you, hurt you or caused you grief. Getting your emotions off your chest and on to the page can express and release your sorrow.

Notes

_____

_____

_____

_____

_____

DECEMBER

6

"Anyone who keeps the ability
to see beauty never grows old."
—Franz Kafka

Want to feel better? If you start feeling impatient, take two minutes to see the beauty in something around you. Whether it's a piece of art, a rose garden or a person you trust, appreciate the beauty they bring to the world.

Notes

_____

_____

_____

_____

_____

DECEMBER

7

"Good memories are our
second chance at happiness."
—Queen Elizabeth II

Photos are our second, and third, and many more chances at happiness. Do you have favorite photos on your digital device? By your desk or bed? Put photos of good times where they'll be in-sight, in-mind so you can keep those happy memories top-of-mind.

Notes

_____

_____

_____

_____

_____

DECEMBER

"Exhaustion is not a status symbol."
—Brene Brown

When people ask how you are, do you say, "Busy?" Instead of seeing exhaustion as a status symbol, what are you going to say instead that articulates how you want to feel?

Notes

_____

_____

_____

_____

_____

DECEMBER

9

"You are only young twice."
—*British TV series*

Would you say you are "young at heart? "Do you feel your age? Act your age? Why or why not?

Notes

_____

_____

_____

_____

_____

DECEMBER

10

"I don't have an empty nest, I have an open nest."
—Sam Horn

Do you know anyone whose kids are out of the house and off leading their own lives? Does this person feel they have an "empty nest?" Could they reframe that to an "open nest?" Their kids aren't "gone," they're doing exactly what they're supposed to be doing at this stage of their life.

Notes

_____

_____

_____

_____

DECEMBER

11

"No more drama."
—Mary J. Blige

Do you know someone who's a "drama queen?" Do they suck you into their drama? Today, could you say, "Count me out. This isn't serving either one of us."

Notes

_____

_____

_____

_____

_____

DECEMBER

12

*"We need to do a better job of putting
ourselves higher on our to-do list."*
—Michelle Obama

How long is your to-do list? Are you anywhere on it? Today, amidst all your
obligations and responsibilities, carve out some time for self-care. What's that
look like to you?

Notes

_____

_____

_____

_____

_____

DECEMBER

13

"Help is the sunny side of control."
—Anne Lamott

What do you think of this provocative quote Anne Lamott shared in her TED talk? Is there someone you're trying to help – and it could actually be a form of control?

Notes

_____

_____

_____

_____

_____

DECEMBER

14

"Have your career and life
become an aircraft carrier?"
—Sam Horn

A navy pilot told me, "Know how you stop an aircraft carrier? You don't. It has so much mass and momentum, it keeps going even after you turn off the engines. "Have you been doing the same thing for so long, you'll keep doing it unless you make a conscious effort to change course?

Notes

_____

_____

_____

_____

_____

DECEMBER

15

"I don't think my story is over yet."
—Serena Williams

When tennis champion Serena Williams discovered she was pregnant during the midst of a Grand Slam run, this is what she said. Have you been working towards something – and life has intervened with other plans? Could you tell yourself, "My story isn't over yet?"

Notes

_____

_____

_____

_____

_____

DECEMBER

16

"You become what you believe."
—Oprah Winfrey

What are three things you know for sure? Do you see how those beliefs have shaped your reality?

Notes

_____

_____

_____

_____

_____

DECEMBER

17

"There is moment in every child's life
where a door opens and lets the future in."
—*Graham Greene*

When did a door open and let your future in? Think back over this year. What was a moment where everything changed – where opportunity knocked and you answered the door?

Notes

_____

_____

_____

_____

_____

DECEMBER

18

*"For most people, the opposite of talking
is not listening, it's waiting."*
—*Fran Leibowitz*

Who is someone who really listens to you? How do they make you feel? How do you feel about that person? Today, put impatience aside and be that listener for someone you care about.

Notes

_____

_____

_____

_____

DECEMBER
19

"The way to resume is to resume.
It is the only way. To resume."
—Gertrude Stein

Do you ever feel like you can't go on? As Gertrude Stein pointed out, resuming is better than wallowing. If you are about to give up on something remind yourself of this. Resume. It is the only way.

Notes

_____

_____

_____

_____

_____

DECEMBER

20

*"If I knew I was going to live this long,
I would have taken better care of myself."*
—*Micky Mantle*

Are you ignoring your body? Promising to take better care of yourself… someday? What is some self-care you can do today? A long bath?

Massage? Walk outside? Get a haircut?

Notes

_____

_____

_____

_____

_____

DECEMBER

21

Lucy: "Do you think anyone ever really changes?"
Linus: "I've changed a lot in the last year."
Lucy: "I mean for the better."
          —Charles M. Schultz

Let's wrap up the last ten days of this year by asking some reflective questions.
Let's look back and ask ourselves how we've changed – for the better. What's one
thing about your life that is better than when you started this year?

Notes

_____

_____

_____

_____

_____

DECEMBER

22

"It's not selfish to put yourself in
your own story; it's smart."
—*Sam Horn*

Would you say you're putting yourself in your own story? How so? When or how do you take yourself out of the story? Why? How will you strike a healthier balance between serving others' needs and your own? What is something you'll do "just for yourself" this week?

Notes

_____

_____

_____

_____

_____

DECEMBER

23

"The real voyage of discovery consists not in seeking new landscapes, but in having new eyes."
—Marcel Proust

In looking back over this year, what did you see with new eyes? What did you discover about life, about your relationships, about yourself?

Notes

_____

_____

_____

_____

_____

DECEMBER

24

"The world was shocked to learn I
wrote a bestseller at 66. No matter how long
you live, you have stories to tell. What else is there to
do but head off on the Conestoga wagon of the soul?"
—Pulitzer Prize winning author Frank McCourt,
Angela's Ashes

Do you think it's too late for you? That the window of opportunity has passed for what you want to do? It's only too late if you don't start… today.

Notes

_____

_____

_____

_____

_____

DECEMBER

25

"The purpose of life is to find your gift.
The meaning is to give it away.
—Pablo Picasso

The best gifts aren't under the Christmas tree. They're your talents, skills, experiences, stories, lessons-learned. How are you leveraging them by giving them away?

Notes

_____

_____

_____

_____

_____

DECEMBER

26

*"When it happens, I want to stop the
match and shout, 'That's what it's all about!'
It's not the big prize I'll win at the end of the match.
It's having done something totally pure, having
experienced the perfect emotion."*
—*Billie Jean King*

Have you experienced this exquisite state of flow? When? Describe what happened, what contributed to you being in the zone, and how it felt.

Notes

_____

_____

_____

_____

_____

DECEMBER

27

*"How we do anything is
how we do everything."*
—Martha Beck

Look back through the pages of this journal. Annie Dillard said, "How we
spend our days is, of course, how we spend our lives." Do you see how what you
do on a daily basis adds up? That every single day accumulates and ultimately
creates the quality of your life?

Notes

_____

_____

_____

_____

_____

DECEMBER

28

*"It is our choices that show us
who we truly are, far more than our abilities."*
—J. K. Rowling

When you reflect on this year, what are three choices that made you happier and healthier?

Notes

_____

_____

_____

_____

_____

DECEMBER

29

*"I think I am quite ready
for another adventure."*
—Bilbo Baggins

What has been a satisfying adventure from this year? Are you ready for another one? What does that look like?

Notes

_____

_____

_____

_____

_____

DECEMBER

30

"I shall tell you a great secret, my friend.
Do not wait for the last judgment.
It takes place every day."
—Albert Camus

Go back through this journal. Did certain memories bring a smile to your heart?
Were you surprised to find you've forgotten some of the things you thought,
said or did? If you learn anything from this journal, please let it be that EVERY
DAY COUNTS.

Notes

_____

_____

_____

_____

_____

DECEMBER

31

"Let us then, be up and doing."
—Longfellow

As we wrap up this year, what will you be up and doing? What will you do to make the most of today, to make the most of this year?

Notes

_____

_____

_____

_____

_____

I HAVE ALWAYS LOVED quotes, ever since I first discovered them in a stack of Readers Digest at my grandparents' house.

The funny, profound one-liners featured throughout those magazines really captured my attention. I started a life-long habit of writing down pearls of wisdom and sharing them in my books and presentations (with attribution, of course).

It is fun riffing off quotes, just as a jazz musician riffs off chords. It's word improv. vDisneyland for the mind and soul.

One of the goals of this journal is to give you opportunities to riff off quotes to facilitate your own epiphanies.

People who have already used this journal said it had a cumulative effect on them. They found themselves being more mindful of how they spent their time. They started taking (and tracking) mini- actions towards their dreams and goals. It helped them be the person they wanted to be.

Rollo May said, "If you do not express your own original ideas, if you do not listen to your own being, you will have betrayed yourself."

This journal is a tangible way to express your own original ideas, listen to your being, reflect, imprint, appreciate, and envision how you want to show up that day. It is a way to speak up for what you want and increase the likelihood of it happening.

I hope this journal has been as joyful and rewarding for you to use as it has been for me to create. Onward.

WHAT'S NEXT

Wondering what's next? Visit www.SamHorn.com for info on our other journals and programs.

We are developing Today, Not Someday… for Writers and a variety of niched journals. Buy one for yourself and gift them to friends, family and team members who want to live their best life.

Interested in a customized program for your organization? We offer a variety of workshops, webinars and inspirational keynotes on how to make the rest of your life the best of your life.

Or, want to attend one of Sam's public events, whether it's an evening salon or a deep-dive weekend?

Contact Cheri@IntrigueAgency to explore how we can work together to deliver your ideal event–or to register for one of our public events.

Want to receive intriguing quotes via text or email? Email us at Sam@IntrigueAgency.com for details about our Quote a Day program.

Check out #SamHornIntrigue on Facebook, Instagram and Twitter to stay updated on when Sam will be in your area and to receive fresh insights on why NOW is the new LATER.

Mark Twain said, "Continuous improvement is better than delayed perfection."

Agreed. Give yourself the gift of continuous improvement. Life can get better and better and better if you make each day count. Best wishes. We look forward to staying connected.

ABOUT SAM HORN

SAM HORN, FOUNDER/CEO OF the Intrigue Agency, is on a mission to help people create a quality life-work that adds value for all involved.

Sam has spoken to more than a half million people worldwide and for such clients as National Geographic, Accenture, Cisco, Boeing, Intel, NASA, Capital One, Nationwide, YPO and National Governors Association.

Her TEDx talks and books–Got Your Attention?, POP!, Tongue Fu! and SOMEDAY is Not a Day in the Week–have been endorsed by Jack Canfield, Stephen Covey, Seth Godin, Tony Robbins, and featured in the New York Times, Forbes, and on NPR.

Sam served as Executive Director of the Maui Writers Conference for 17 years and as Pitch Coach for Springboard Enterprises which has helped women entrepreneurs recieve $8.8 billion in funding.

In 2015, Sam took Paulo Coelho's quote–"One day, you're going to wake up and there won't be anytime left to do the things you've always wanted to do" — to heart.

She took her business on the road for a Year by the Water where she visited "bucket list" places including Walden's Pond, Monet's Garden and Helen Keller's water pump.

Along the way, she learned we CAN have the best of both worlds. We can make a good LIVING doing work we love with people we enjoy and respect–and make a good LIFE by doing what's important to us NOW, not someday.

Sam is a woman on a mission and welcomes opportunities to share her inspiring message with people so they are motivated to make the rest of their life the best of their life.

Want to stay connected with Sam? Visit www.SamHorn.com to learn about her SOMEDAY salons, public workshops, other books/journals and to subscribe to her newsletter to find out when she'll be speaking in your area.

And contact Sam's Business Manager Cheri Grimm at Cheri@IntrigueAgency. com to arrange for Sam to share her inspiring keynote with your group

Made in the USA
Middletown, DE
17 January 2020